5th

Social Studies

Daily Practice Workbook
20 weeks of fun activities

ARGOPREP

History

Government

Geography

Economics

ArgoPrep is one of the leading providers of supplemental educational products and services. We offer affordable and effective test prep solutions to educators, parents and students. Learning should be fun and easy! To access more resources visit us at www.argoprep.com.

Our goal is to make your life easier, so let us know how we can help you by e-mailing us at: info@argoprep.com.

- ArgoPrep is a recipient of the prestigious **Mom's Choice Award**.

- ArgoPrep also received the 2019 **Seal of Approval** from Homeschool.com for our award-winning workbooks.

- ArgoPrep was awarded the 2019 **National Parenting Products Award**, **Gold Medal Parent's Choice Award** and **the Tillywig Brain Child Award.**

SOCIAL STUDIES

Social Studies Daily Practice Workbook by ArgoPrep allows students to build foundational skills and review concepts. Our workbooks explore social studies topics in depth with ArgoPrep's 5 E's to build social studies mastery.

OTHER BOOKS BY ARGOPREP

Here are some other test prep workbooks by ArgoPrep you may be interested in. All of our workbooks come equipped with detailed video explanations to make your learning experience a breeze! Visit us at *www.argoprep.com*

COMMON CORE MATH SERIES

COMMON CORE ELA SERIES

INTRODUCING MATH!

Introducing Math! by ArgoPrep is an award-winning series created by certified teachers to provide students with high-quality practice problems. Our workbooks include topic overviews with instruction, practice questions, answer explanations along with digital access to video explanations. Practice in confidence - with ArgoPrep!

SCIENCE SERIES

Science Daily Practice Workbook by ArgoPrep is an award-winning series created by certified science teachers to help build mastery of foundational science skills. Our workbooks explore science topics in depth with ArgoPrep's 5 E'S to build science mastery.

KIDS SUMMER ACADEMY SERIES

ArgoPrep's Kids Summer Academy series helps prevent summer learning loss and gets students ready for their new school year by reinforcing core foundations in math, english and science. Our workbooks also introduce new concepts so students can get a head start and be on top of their game for the new school year!

CAPTAIN BRAVERY

WATER FIRE

MYSTICAL NINJA

GREEN POISON

FIRESTORM WARRIOR

RAPID NINJA

CAPTAIN ARGO

THUNDER WARRIOR

ADRASTOS THE SUPER WARRIOR

DANCE HERO

GREEN DRAGON WARRIOR

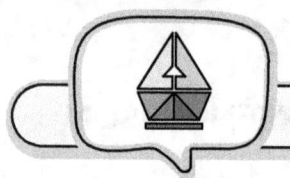

Table of Contents

Introduction

Welcome to our fifth-grade social studies workbook! This workbook has been specifically designed to help students build mastery of foundational social studies skills that are taught in fifth grade. Included are 20 weeks of comprehensive instruction covering the history and geography of the Western Hemisphere. Students will learn more about the cultures, civilizations, and empires; interaction between societies; and the comparison of the government and economic systems of modern nations.

This workbook covers seven key ideas:

EARLY PEOPLES OF THE AMERICAS: The first humans in the Western Hemisphere modified their physical environment as well as adapted to their environment. Their interactions with their environment led to various innovations and to the development of unique cultures.

COMPLEX SOCIETIES AND CIVILIZATIONS: Between 1100 B.C.E. and 1500 C.E, complex societies and civilizations developed in the Western Hemisphere. Although these complex societies and civilizations have certain defining characteristics in common, each is also known for unique cultural achievements and contributions.

EUROPEAN EXPLORATION AND ITS EFFECTS: Various European powers explored and eventually colonized the Western Hemisphere. This had a profound effect on Native Americans and led to the transatlantic slave trade.

GEOGRAPHY IN THE WESTERN HEMISPHERE: The diverse geography of the Western Hemisphere has influenced human culture and settlement in distinct ways. Human communities in the Western Hemisphere have modified the physical environment.

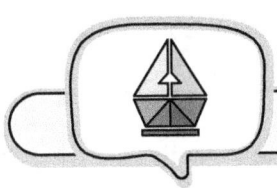
COMPARATIVE CULTURES: The countries of the Western Hemisphere are diverse and the cultures of these countries are rich and varied. Due to their proximity to each other, the countries of the Western Hemisphere share some of the same concerns and issues.

GOVERNMENT: The political systems of the Western Hemisphere vary in structure and organization across time and place.

ECONOMICS: The peoples of the Western Hemisphere have developed various ways to meet their needs and wants. Many of the countries of the Western Hemisphere trade with each other, as well as with other countries around the world.

This workbook also includes detailed video explanations going over every page and question in the workbook. To access video explanations, visit **argoprep.com/social5**

How to Use the Book

All 20 weeks of daily activity pages in the book follow the same weekly structure. The activities in each of the sections align to the recommendations of the National Council for the Social Studies which will help prepare students for state standardized assessments. While the sections can be completed in any order, it is important to complete each week within the section in chronological order since the skills often build upon one another.

Each week focuses on one specific topic within the section. More information about the weekly structure can be found in the Weekly Planner section.

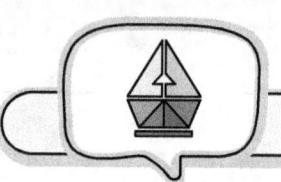
Weekly Planner

Day	Activity	Description
1	Engaging with the Topic	Read a short text on the topic and answer multiple choice questions.
2	Exploring the Topic	Interact with the topic on a deeper level by collecting, analyzing and interpreting information.
3	Explaining the Topic	Make sense of the topic by explaining and beginning to draw conclusions about information.
4	Experiencing the Topic	Investigate the topic by making real-life connections.
5	Elaborating on the Topic	Reflect on the topic and use all information learned to draw conclusions and evaluate results.

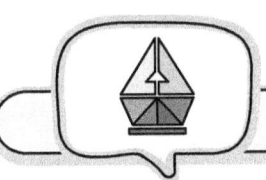
List of Topics

Unit	Week	Topic
Geography and Individual Development	1	The First People in the Americas
Geography and Individual Development	2	Settling the Americas
Individual Development	3	Complex Societies and Civilizations
History and Economics	4	European Exploration and Conquest
Exchange	5	The Columbian Exchange
Exchange	6	The Middle Passage
Geography	7	Geography of North America
Individual Development	8	Immigration and Culture in the United States
Individual Development	9	Canadian Culture
Individual Development	10	Latin American Culture
Geography	11	Environmental Issues in the Western Hemisphere
Government	12	Founding the United States
Government	13	The Government of the United States
Civics and Government	14	Governments in the Western Hemisphere
Time, Change, and Continuity	15	The Civil Rights Movement
Time, Change, and Continuity	16	The Women's Rights Movement
Government and Civics	17	Multinational Organizations
History and Economics	18	Economies of the Western Hemisphere
Geography and Economics	19	Natural Resources in the Western Hemisphere
Economics	20	The Importance of Trade

Geography and Individual Development

The First People in the Americas

This week you will learn about the First Peoples in the Americas and how they lived.

ARGOPREP

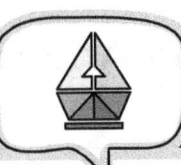
Directions: Read the text below. Then answer the questions that follow.

Native Americans, also called **First Peoples**, believe that they have been in the Americas "since time immemorial." That means a really long time! Archeologists have found a lot of evidence that supports this belief. The oldest evidence of humans as far south as Mexico is a pair of fossilized footprints dating back to 22,000 years ago. Archaeologists collect old artifacts from all around North and South America in order to piece together a timeline of when people started occupying the Americas. Based on all of their evidence, there are two competing theories on how exactly they arrived. The first is the **Bering Land Bridge** hypothesis, which states that, around 30,000 years ago, during the Ice Age, there was a narrow bridge of land between Asia and North America, connecting modern-day Russia and Alaska. Many historians believe that early peoples crossed this land bridge in search of more food, and slowly made their way south over thousands of years. The second theory is that early peoples made their way across that same area, also around 30,000 years ago, but with boats, and sailed down the coasts of North and South America. We may never know which theory is correct. What we do know is that Native Americans have been in the Americas for a very long time.

1. How old are the fossilized footprints in Mexico?

   A. 15,000 years old

   B. 22,000 years old

   C. 30,000 years old

   D. 45,00 years old

2. About how long ago did the first humans arrive in North America?

   A. 15,000 years ago

   B. 22,000 years ago

   C. 30,000 years ago

   D. 45,000 years ago

3. What two places did the Bering Land Bridge connect?

   A. Alaska and Quebec

   B. Alaska and Russia

   C. Russia and California

   D. Alaska and Canada

4. From what continent did the First Peoples most likely come to North America?

   A. Australia

   B. Africa

   C. Europe

   D. Asia

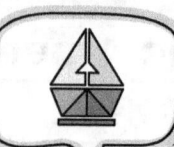
Directions: Read the text below. Then answer the questions that follow.

"

It is possible that human arrival in the Americas occurred by both land and sea routes. Both theories of human arrival in the Americas agree that people originating from Asia moved steadily south upon arrival in the Americas, first occupying what is now Alaska and Canada, then spreading south and east into what is now the United States, Central America, and South America.

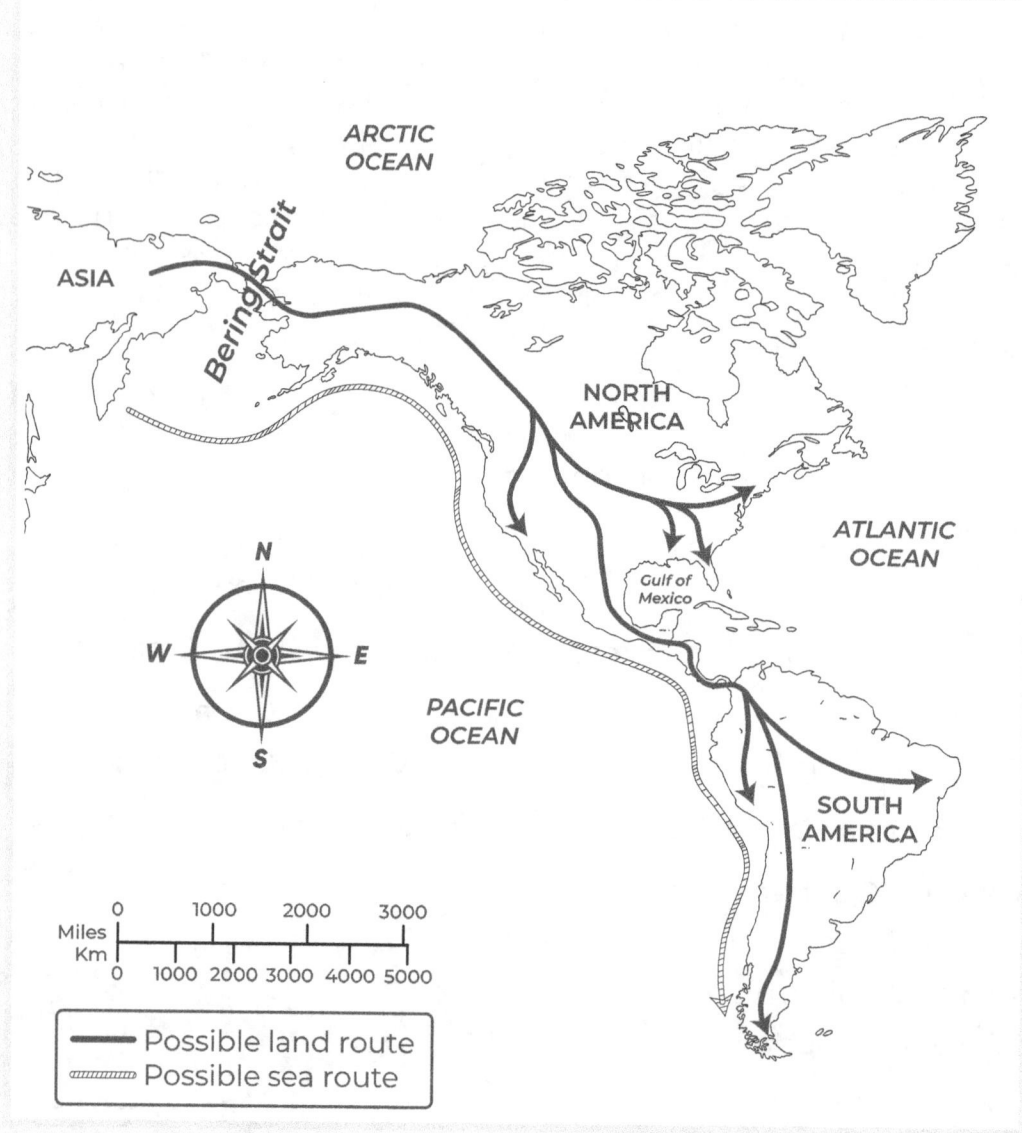

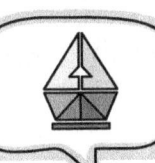
1. Which general direction did the First Peoples travel in?

    A. North

    B. South

    C. East

    D. West

2. Which body of water may the First Peoples have traveled across?

    A. Arctic Ocean

    B. Atlantic Ocean

    C. Gulf of Mexico

    D. Pacific Ocean

3. List three modern-day countries in North, Central, and South America that the First Peoples occupied.

    A. ....

    B. ....

    C. ....

4. Using the scale on the map, estimate how many miles the First Peoples may have traveled from their start in Asia to the bottom of South America.

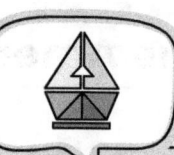
Directions: Read the text below. Then answer the questions that follow.

The First Peoples to come to the Americas likely did so for survival purposes. These people were **hunter-gatherers**, which means they hunted animals and gathered other food like berries, nuts, mushrooms, and plants to eat. These people were very skilled at hunting and could take down wooly mammoths and other giant animals with just their spears. In fact, many historians believe that it was these large animals that the First Peoples followed across the Bering Land Bridge. However, hunting could be dangerous, difficult, and unpredictable, so they had to also rely on their skills of identifying and collecting plants and mushrooms for more than half of their diet.

Because hunter-gatherers followed their food in order to survive, they are considered **nomadic**. To be nomadic means to always be on the move. When you are always on the move, you do not build permanent homes or cities. You also do not **domesticate**, or train, animals to stay in one place, the way farmers do, in order to get food from them. The First Peoples did not need to do any of this because they were skilled at surviving as hunter-gatherers. If they had not been so good at surviving on the move, they would not have been able to spread across the Americas, as far south as the tip of South America.

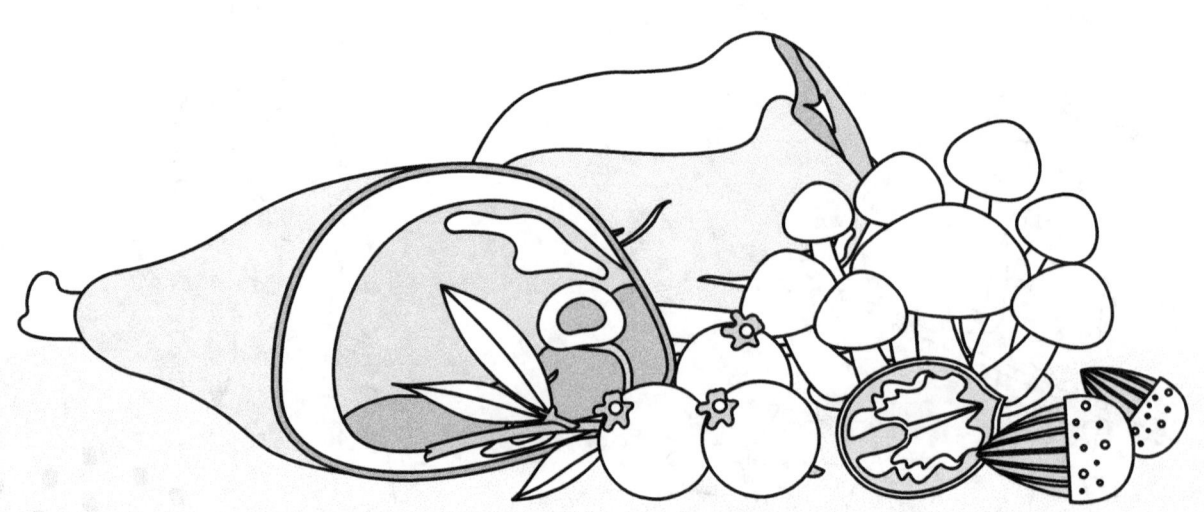

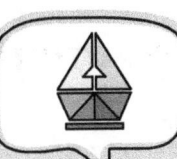
1. Why did hunter-gatherers rely mostly on berries, nuts, mushrooms, and other plants for most of their diet?

....

....

....

2. Why were hunter-gatherers nomadic?

....

....

3. Name two benefits of domesticating animals:

A. ....

B. ....

4. Why were the First Peoples able to travel all the way to South America?

....

....

....

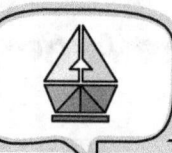
Directions: Read the text below and follow the instructions provided to complete the activity.

The First Peoples of the Americas had to be very skilled at remembering exactly where certain plants and animals could be found. There is no evidence of paper or writing from this time, so it is likely they had to remember it all in their heads! Go out for a walk at the nearest park or in your backyard and look for different foods that you could eat to survive if you were a hunter-gatherer. In the space below, draw a map of your travels, labeling places where you could hunt, gather, and sleep. Label where you found any wild foods, like mushrooms, nuts, or berries.

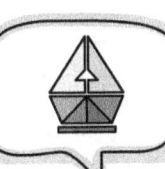
Directions: Read the text below. Then answer the questions that follow.

This week you've learned about how the First Peoples of the Americas may have reached the continents and how they would have survived. Using this knowledge, answer the following questions.

1. What might have been the most difficult parts of being a hunter-gatherer? Think of at least three examples.

....

....

....

2. Would you rather be a hunter-gatherer or a farmer with domesticated animals? Support your answer with details from the readings.

....

....

....

3. Why do you think the First Peoples were nomadic for so long? What benefits might there be to a nomadic lifestyle?

....

....

....

....

WEEK 2

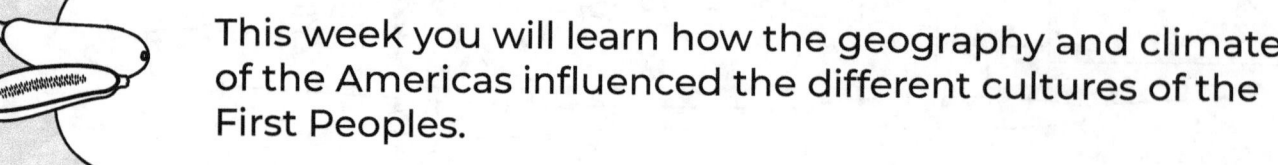

This week you will learn how the geography and climate of the Americas influenced the different cultures of the First Peoples.

ARGOPREP

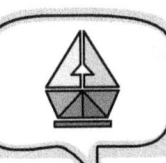
Directions: Read the text below. Then answer the questions that follow.

"

The First Peoples of the Americas did not stay in one place. As they hunted herds of animals, they gradually moved further south and east over thousands of years until they were dispersed across all of the Americas. Around 11,000 years ago, with the end of the Ice Age, the ice melted and the ocean rose, covering up the Bering Land Bridge. As a result of warmer temperatures, some of the larger animals like the wooly mammoths were going extinct, and the First Peoples started hunting smaller animals instead, such as bears and deer. One advantage of the warmer temperatures after the Ice Age was the ability to plant and grow food in the fertile soil. Over time, these First Peoples who were once nomadic began to live their lives in permanent settlements across the Americas, usually settling near rivers or other bodies of water. Some groups settled in colder **climates**, like in Canada and Alaska, while others settled in warmer climates, like in the Rocky Mountains of North America, or the deserts and rainforests of Central and South America. The different climates of these regions, along with the resources they provided, led to many distinct **cultures**, or ways of life, across the Americas.

"

1. Why did the Bering Land Bridge no longer exist?

    A. destroyed by earthquakes   **C.** a warmer climate

    B. eroded by hurricanes   **D.** a cooler climate

2. What was one advantage that came along with the end of the Ice Age?

    A. no more wooly mammoths   **C.** a colder climate

    B. fertile soil for planting   **D.** dry deserts

3. Where did people usually settle?

    A. near water   **C.** near canyons

    B. near forests   **D.** near land bridges

4. What word means a people's way of life?

    A. custom

    B. culture

    C. climate

    D. settlements

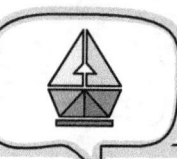
Directions: Read the text below. Then answer the questions that follow.

Over thousands of years, as the First Peoples spread across the Americas, they grew into distinct cultures, each with their own unique ways of life. Read through the chart below to learn about some of the different cultures of the First Peoples, also known as Native Americans, in North America.

Region	Culture
Arctic	In the cold Northern regions of the Arctic, people lived in houses made from whale bone and sod. They built igloos to sleep in during hunting trips. They hunted polar bears, seals, and otters, harpooned whales, and fished with kayaks to make up most of their diet.
Northeast	In the woodlands of the Northeast, people lived in longhouses made of timber. They hunted animals, and harvested fruits, nuts, and other plants from throughout the forest. They often cared for certain plots of land in order to return to them yearly to harvest.
Southeast	In the Southeast, people lived in houses made of woven cane, reeds, and wood. They farmed the fertile soil, growing maize (corn), beans, squash, and sunflower. They also fished in the rivers and hunted game to supplement their diet.
Plains	On the Plains, people lived in tipis that they could take down and move from place to place as they followed herds of animals like buffalo to hunt. Some tribes were not entirely nomadic and did some farming as well.
Great Basin	In this rocky, arid region between the Plains and the West Coast, people were mostly nomadic. They lived in small tents made from tree branches and animal skins, which they could easily move from place to place. They gathered roots, nuts, and other plants, and hunted lizards, snakes, and game.
Southwest	In the deserts of the Southwest, people carved elaborate cave homes into the cliffs, or built pueblos, which were made of baked mud bricks called adobe. Some of the villages were quite large and had gardens to grow food. They also hunted and gathered.
Pacific Northwest	In the rainy forests of the Pacific Northwest, many people built permanent settlements along the rivers and the coast, where they would fish for salmon, and gather roots, berries, nuts, and other plants from seasonal plots of land. They also hunted for game in the forests.

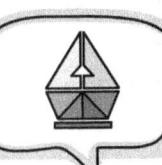
1. In which cultural region were the people mostly nomadic?

A. Arctic

B. Southeast

C. Great Basin

D. Pacific Northwest

2. How did the climate and geography of each region affect its culture? Explain your thinking. Use evidence from the chart to support your answer.

....

....

....

....

....

3. Why do you think some cultures were more nomadic than others? Use what you have learned in previous lessons to support your thinking.

....

....

....

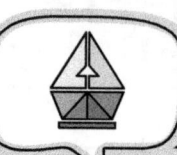
Directions: Read the text below. Then answer the questions that follow.

As the unique cultural regions in the Americas continued to develop, people banded together in groups, called **tribes**, with their own governments, languages, and distinct cultures.

The Iroquois were a collection of multiple tribes who lived in the northeastern woodlands of what is today the United States. They practiced a form of farming that required seasonal burning in the forest. This helped make the soil more fertile, and caused some of the trees to grow more nuts to eat. The open meadows in the forest resulting from the fires also created good places to hunt animals, since the animals were drawn into these open plots of land to eat the nuts from the trees and the other vegetables that people planted there. The Iroquois planted crops like maize (corn), beans, and squash, which together they called the "**Three Sisters**." They called them this because they grew them all together, in mounds of dirt, rather than separately, in rows. The maize provided something for the beans to climb, the roots of the beans provided essential nutrients for the soil, and the large leaves of the squash kept the soil from drying out in the sun. The Iroquois lived in longhouses that could house several families at once, in large villages. The many tribes of the Iroquois shared one government, which would later become a model for the United States.

The Inuit people lived in the extremely cold Arctic climate in what is today Alaska and Northern Canada. To keep warm, they would build houses made of stone or whale bones which were then covered with earth. They would also build igloos out of ice while on hunting trips in order to keep warm. They traveled across the tops of the snow with snowshoes, and down the rivers and in the ocean in kayaks. The animals that they hunted included caribou, polar bears, walruses, seals, whales, and fish. They never wasted any part of an animal, using it for food, clothing, shelter, and tools. They didn't have a large, central government like the Iroquois, so it was mainly up to the smaller family groups to determine the rules for their people.

The Taino people lived in the tropical climate of the Caribbean in areas such as modern day Cuba and Puerto Rico. The Taino lived in villages and used farming to harvest crops like yams, maize, and beans, while also using seasonal burning methods similar to the Iroquois. As opposed to the Inuit and Iroquois, the Taino hunted much smaller animals like snakes and birds. Their homes were round and made of wooden poles which were covered in straw and leaves. Very little clothing was needed due to the warm climate. Taino villages were usually led by a chief, and this chief was usually determined by bloodlines. Being a chief was usually passed down from father to son. Chiefs would have the final say when it came to governance and law making.

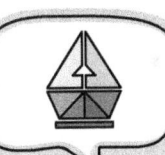
1. Which group's government system is most like that of the United States today?

....

2. What method of farming was used by both the Iroquois and the Taino?

....

3. Choose one group from this section and explain how the climate or geography of their region affected their way of life.

....

....

....

....

....

....

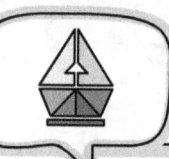
Directions: Read the text below. Then answer the questions that follow.

Native Americans used to have settlements in the place where you live today. Using an online search engine, research information on the Native American tribes that lived in your area. What was their culture like in the past?

Name of the tribe	
Climate and geography of the region	
Types of houses they built	
What they hunted and farmed	
Type of government	
Language	
Ceremonies and Traditions	

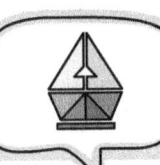
1. After filling in the chart, write a 4-5 sentence paragraph summarizing the culture of the tribe you researched. Include in your paragraph how the climate and geography of the region affected their culture.

....

....

....

....

....

....

....

....

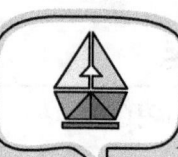
Directions: Read the text below. Then follow the directions to complete the activity.

This week you learned about many different groups that settled all over the Americas. You learned about the different ways of living in various parts of the Americas. Select two cultural regions from the following list to fill out the diagram below. In the outer circles, write some unique characteristics for each cultural region. Where the circles overlap, write what the cultural regions had in common. Choose two: the Arctic, the Northeast, the Southeast, the Plains, the Great Basin, the Southwest, the Pacific Northwest, or the Caribbean.

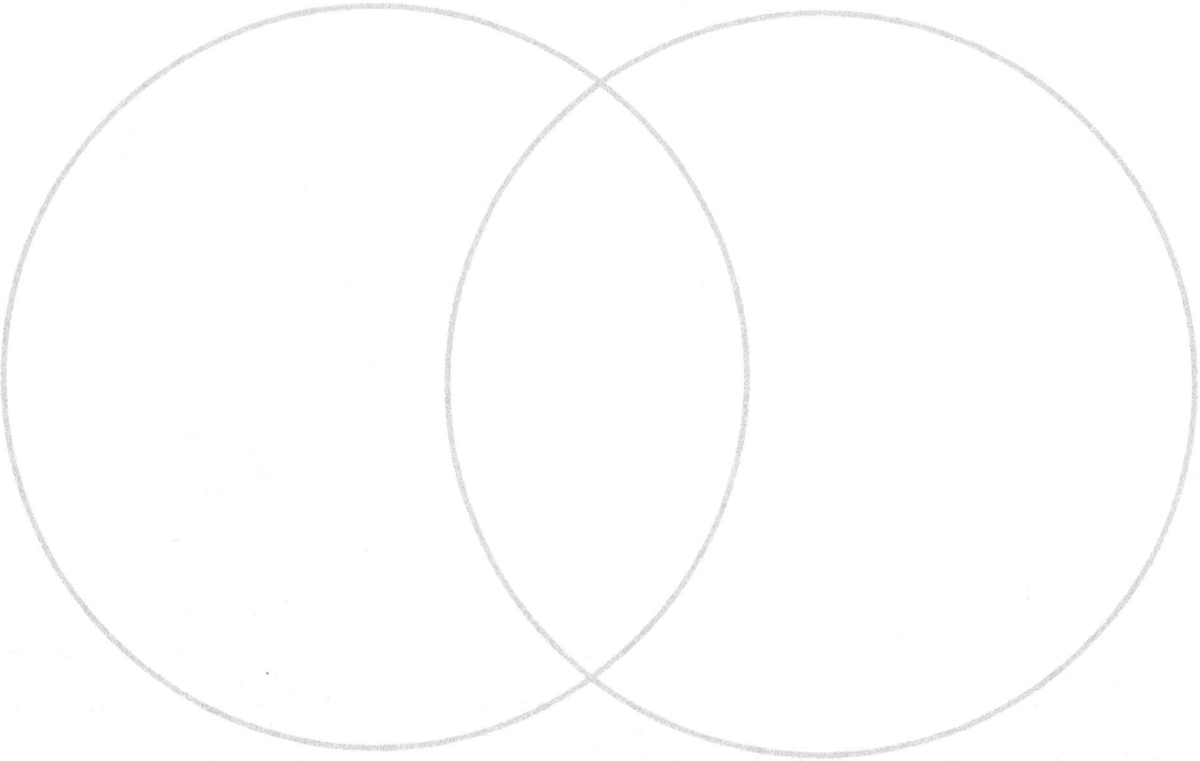

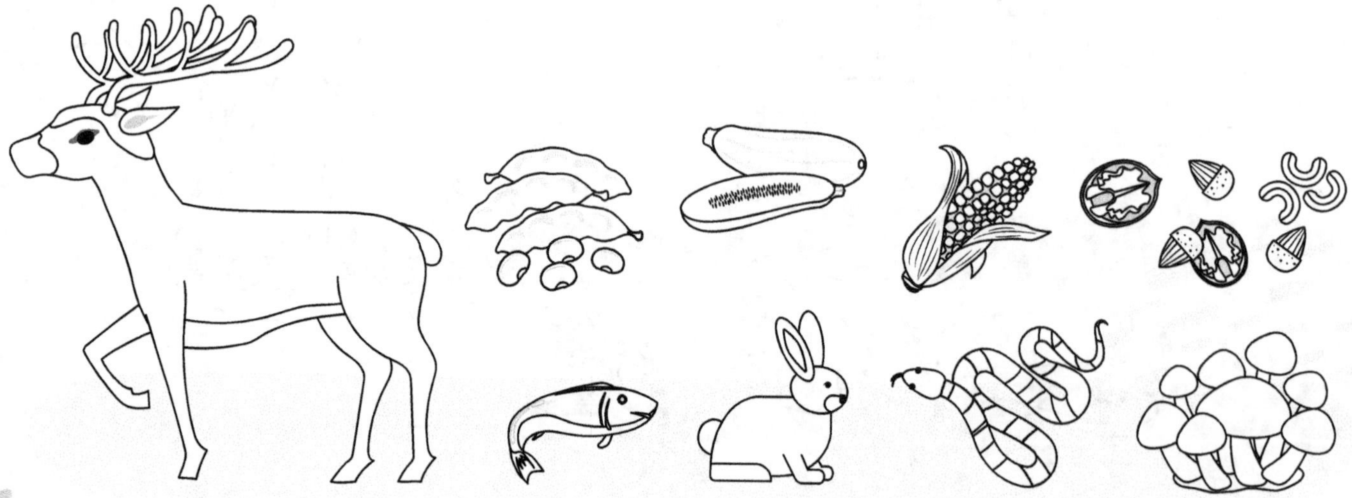

WEEK 3

Individual Development

Complex Societies and Civilizations

This week you will learn how civilizations are developed and compare several ancient civilizations of the Americas.

ARGOPREP

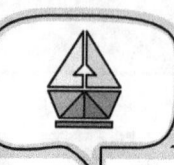
Directions: Read the text below. Then answer the questions that follow.

> Four of the oldest **civilizations**, or complex societies, in the Americas, were the Olmec, Maya, Inca, and Aztec. These civilizations were located in what is now Central and South America. Civilizations occur when many people who share a common language and culture live together in one area, often under the same system of government. Historians believe that the rise of **agriculture**, or large-scale farming, led to the beginning of large civilizations. When a group of people become successful at agriculture, it means that they can stay in one place, instead of hunting and gathering. This leads to the building of permanent towns. Another result of becoming successful at agriculture is something called a **surplus**, which means extra food. When people don't have to worry about what they will eat every day, they can store away the surplus for the winter, use it to help feed their neighbors, or trade it with neighboring civilizations for other goods. This allows people to focus on other things, like learning to write, make art, clothing, and complex tools, building large cities, and forming governments for protection. This is how big civilizations are built up slowly over time.

1. What is a civilization?

   A. a town   **C.** a complex society

   B. a city   **D.** a country

2. What is the main factor that caused the rise in civilizations?

   A. language   **C.** agriculture

   B. culture   **D.** government

3. What is agriculture?

   A. large-scale farming   **C.** a shared language

   B. large-scale governments   **D.** a shared culture

4. Which of the following is NOT a benefit of a surplus?

   A. you can store it for later

   B. you can use it to make tools

   C. you can share it with others

   D. you can trade it for other goods

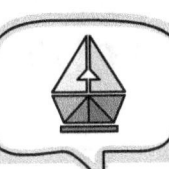
Directions: Read the text below. Then answer the questions that follow.

The Olmec, Aztec, Maya, and Inca civilizations of the Americas all had their own unique language, art, and government, due to their different cultures and geographic regions.

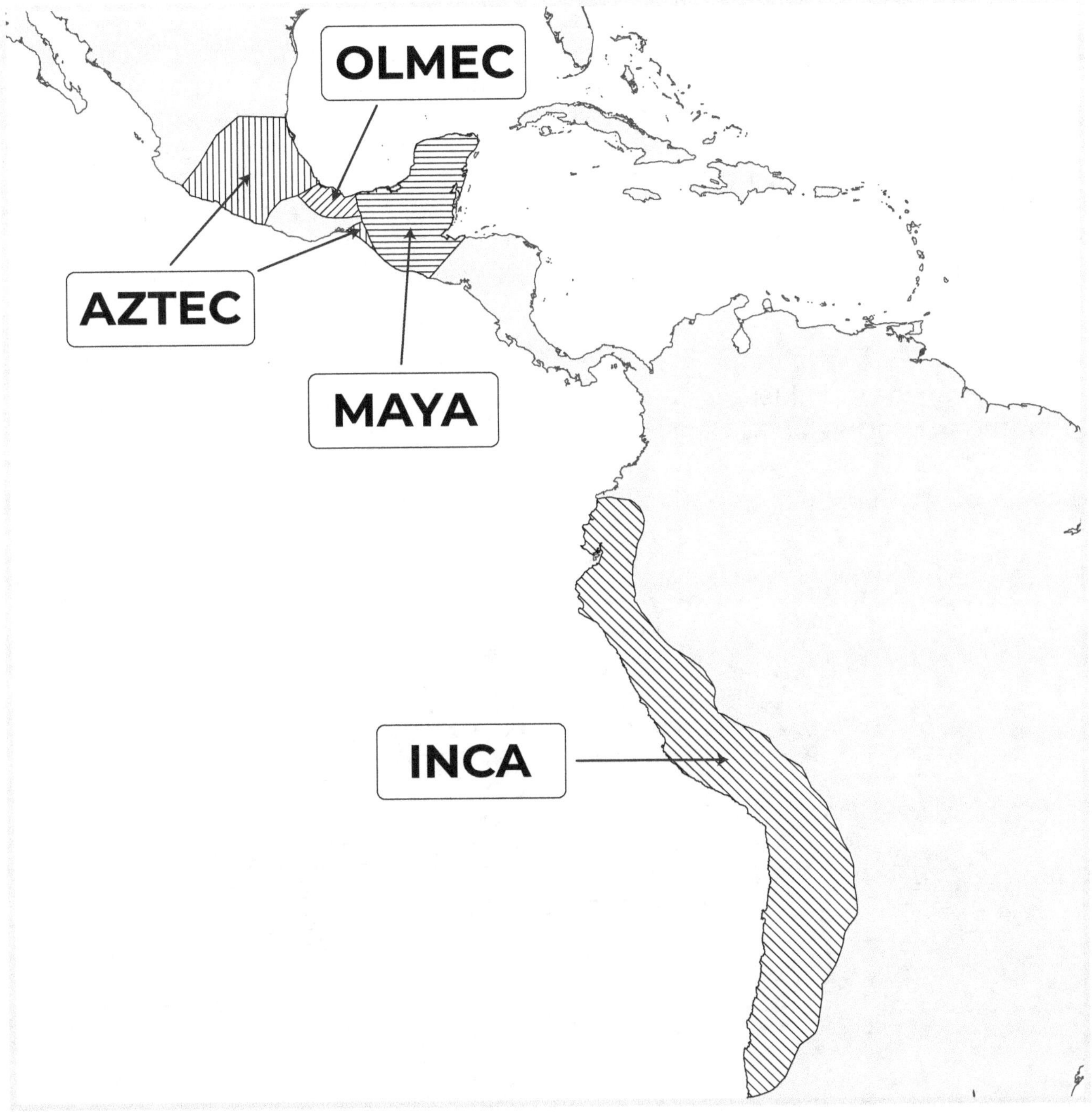

OLMEC

AZTEC

MAYA

INCA

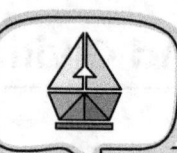
The Olmec

The Olmec civilization was settled around 1500 BCE in what is now southern Mexico. The Olmec civilization included multiple cities that each served a unique purpose. Some cities focused on agriculture, and their crops fed most of the civilization. Other cities focused on mining natural minerals like jade and obsidian. These were used for building and making art and other tools. The Olmec also traded their surplus crops and minerals with neighboring civilizations. **Trade** benefits both civilizations involved by allowing them to not only exchange goods, but also ideas. It was through trade with other civilizations that the Olmec spread their culture and influence throughout the entire region. Religion was a very important part of life for the Olmec, and their **architecture**, or building style, showed that. Their architecture influenced other nearby civilizations. For example, the building style shown in the image below is found throughout what is now southern Mexico, not just within the Olmec civilization.

This pyramid was influenced
by the architecture of the Olmecs.

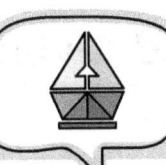
Look at the image on the previous page and answer the following questions based on what you have learned.

1. Describe the pyramid in your own words.

....

....

....

....

2. Knowing that the Olmec buried their leaders in these pyramids, what does that tell you about their leaders?

....

....

....

....

....

....

3. What can these pyramids tell you about the Olmec religion?

....

....

....

....

4. How did the Olmec spread their culture?

    A. trade

    B. government

    C. religion

    D. architecture

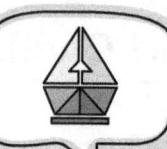
Directions: Read the text below. Then answer the questions that follow.

The Maya

The Maya settled on the Yucatan Peninsula in what is now southern Mexico around the year 300. The Maya used **glyphs**, or symbols, carved into stone to record their history, mainly writing about the achievements of their rulers. The Maya were able to grow tremendous amounts of food using advanced agricultural techniques, and they frequently traded and waged war with groups around them. They possessed no wheels or animals for transportation but instead relied on enslaved people or boats to carry items from place to place. The Maya were deeply curious about the stars and built elaborate temples and observatories to observe the sky. Based on their observations, they made an accurate calendar that influences the one we use today. Religion was important to the Maya and their religious leaders were the most powerful people in their society. These leaders made the most important decisions for all of their people.

The Maya often created paintings and sculptures to celebrate their gods. At its peak, the Mayan civilization had around 40 cities, each with a population of 5,000 to 500,000 people. The houses in these cities were usually made of mud or stone with straw roofs. The cities also had streets, shops, plazas, and big buildings like palaces and temples.

The Inca

The Inca civilization spread across 2,000 miles in the Andes Mountains, in what is now Peru and parts of Chile, in South America. They established their capital city Cuzco in the 1100s and continued to grow to a civilization of 12 million people by the 1500s. The Inca built incredible cities that included canals, roads, and bridges. Their buildings were typically made of stone, as were their houses. Perhaps what was most amazing about the Inca was that their farmers grew about half as many types of foods as are grown all over the world today. They used **irrigation**, digging canals to bring water to the fields, to increase their crop production. Another farming technique they used was called **step farming**, carving large flat plots of land into the sides of mountains, in order to increase the amount of space they had to grow food. Foods like tomatoes, squash, potatoes, and peppers were all essential parts of the Incan diet. Animals like llamas and

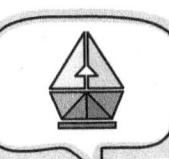
alpacas helped with manual labor and transportation, especially in transporting goods to and from the city of Machu Picchu, located high in the Andes mountains. The Inca were ruled by a single **monarch**, or king, called the Sapa Inca. This person made all of the decisions for all people within the empire. The government kept careful records of everything going on in the civilization. They used **quipus**, a counting device made out of strings, to track everything from population to crop yields.

The Aztec

After the Maya declined around 900 CE, another group known as the Toltec emerged. The Toltec mined obsidian glass and used it to make weapons. They traded the obsidian glass to other groups as well, giving them great power over their neighbors. Around the year 1200, the Aztec moved into the region that was occupied by the Toltec and conquered them. Similar to the Inca, the Aztec built temples, roads, and bridges. The temples looked much like the Olmec temples from the same region. The Aztec were ruled by a monarch, who they believed was chosen by the gods, giving him the divine right to rule. Their homes were built with bricks made from mud. The largest city, Tenochtitlan, was built on an island in the middle of a lake and had a population of 400,000 people. Since they were on a lake, farmers built **floating gardens** to grow crops. A floating garden, or chinampa, is a collection of floating rafts, covered with soil, and used as garden beds to grow crops. This technique helped the plants get the water they needed without having to be watered by hand.

1. What did the Maya use to record their history?

   A. books

   B. paintings

   C. glyphs

   D. quipus

2. How was irrigation important for the Inca?

....

....

....

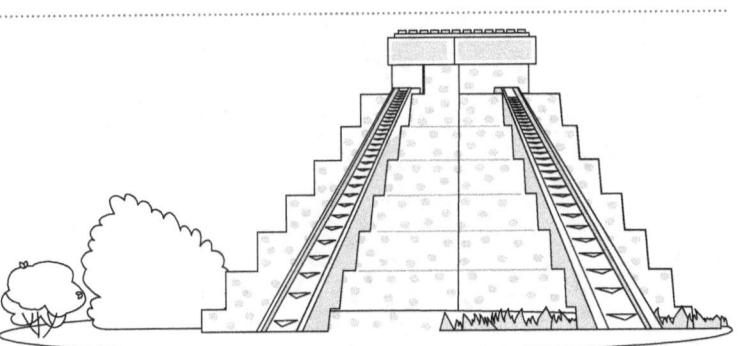

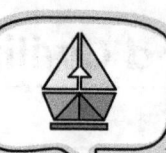
3. Draw a picture of either a floating garden or a step farm in the space provided below. Label the different parts based on what you learned in the reading.

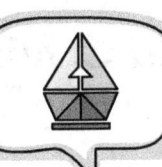
Directions: Read the text below. Then answer the question that follows.

There are many things to consider when choosing a place you would like to live for the rest of your life. If you had to choose an early society to be a part of, which would it be? Using what you have learned about the Maya, Inca, and Aztec, create a well-developed paragraph below. Include information about what type of house you would live in, the type of job you might like to do, and any other information that would be useful in explaining your decision.

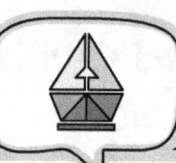
Directions: Read the text below. Then follow the directions to complete the activity.

This week you have learned about the Maya, the Inca, and the Aztec. Each civilization shared many similarities, but also had many differences. Using the information you learned this week and the internet for any additional information, fill in the chart below to the best of your ability.

Feature	Maya	Inca	Aztec
Type of Government			
Farming			
Type of Shelter			
Location			
Transportation			

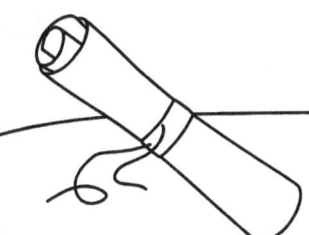

WEEK 4

History and Economics

European Exploration and Conquest

This week you will learn about the actions that Europeans took to conquer the Americas and how this affected the lives of Native Americans and Africans.

ARGOPREP

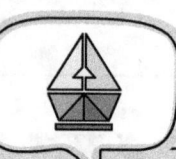
Directions: Read the text below. Then answer the questions that follow.

> After the voyages of Christopher Columbus, European nations quickly became interested in exploring and settling the Americas. After Columbus completed his voyages, Vasco Núñez de Balboa set sail from Portugal. He became the first European to see the Pacific Ocean from the Americas. Another famous explorer was Ferdinand Magellan, who set sail from Spain. Magellan became the first person to ever **circumnavigate**, or sail all the way around, the world. The Spanish also sent soldiers to the Americas led by men called **conquistadors**, or conquerors, to investigate and conquer Central and South America for Spain. One conquistador was Hernán Cortés, who conquered the Aztec in 1521, ending their empire. Cortés and his soldiers were able to conquer the Aztec not only through warfare but also through the transmission of diseases. More Aztec people died from European diseases than from warfare. Another conquistador, Francisco Pizarro, was looking to take the Inca Empire's gold and silver supplies and conquered them in 1532. Many Europeans from countries like England, France, and the Netherlands also completed several voyages to claim new lands and establish **colonies** in the Americas. A colony is a settlement of people from one country who moved to another place to claim the land for their home country. In the process of European countries gaining control of land in the Americas through conquistadors and colonies, the majority of the Native Americans died from disease. A smaller percentage died from warfare. Those who survived had their lands taken from them by the Europeans who gained control of the land, and were forced to give up their religious and cultural traditions.

1. Who was the first explorer to circumnavigate the globe?

   A. Christopher Columbus

   B. Vasco Núñez de Balboa

   C. Ferdinand Magellan

   D. Hernán Cortés

2. Which country sent conquistadors to conquer land in the Americas?

   A. England

   B. Portugal

   C. France

   D. Spain

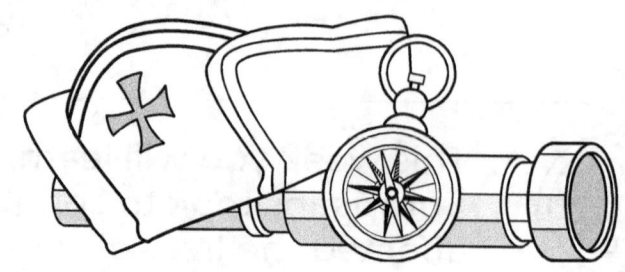

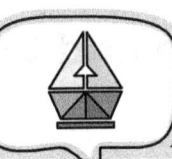
3. Who conquered the Inca Empire?

    A. Vasco Núñez de Balboa

    B. Ferdinand Magellan

    C. Hernán Cortés

    D. Francisco Pizarro

4. What happened to the majority of the Indigenous people when the conquistadors came to Central and South America?

    A. They died from disease.

    B. They died from warfare.

    C. They had their land taken away.

    D. They had to convert to a new religion.

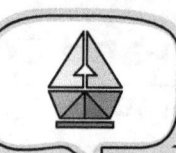
Directions: Read the text below. Then answer the questions that follow.

The conquest of the Americas by European nations was a gradual process that lasted several hundred years. Examine the timeline below to learn more about which explorers claimed land for their countries. When you are done, answer the questions that follow.

Christopher Columbus lands on Hispaniola
1492

Magellan begins circumnavigating the globe
1519

Pizarro conquers the Inca Empire for Spain
1532

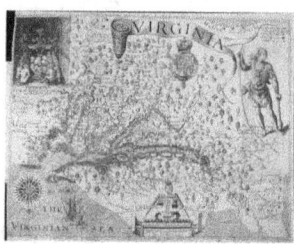

First permanent English settlement founded at Jamestown
1607

1494
Treaty of Tordesillas between Spain and Portugal allows Spain to conquer most of Central and South America and Portugal to conquer Brazil.

1521
Hernán Cortés conquers the Aztec Empire for Spain

1603
Samuel de Champlain founds New France

1624
The Dutch found New Amsterdam on Manhattan Island

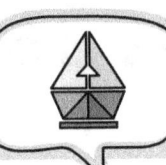
1. How many years passed between Columbus landing on Hispaniola and the first Permanent English settlement at Jamestown?

....

2. Which European countries had a presence in the Americas according to this timeline?

....

....

3. The Treaty of Tordesillas was an agreement between Spain and Portugal about who could conquer what lands all over the world. Do you think this agreement was fair to people who were not Portuguese or Spanish? Explain your thinking.

....

....

....

....

....

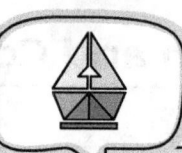
Directions: Read the text below. Then answer the questions that follow.

The Spanish financed the very first set of voyages to the Americas by paying for Christopher Columbus's expeditions. However, some of their most noteworthy journeys came a few decades later when various conquistadors conquered the Aztecs and the Incas. By taking over critical areas in Central, North, and South America, as well as in the modern-day Caribbean, Spain was able to build a vast empire. At the same time, the Portuguese built their empire mainly in modern day Brazil, in South America, while the Dutch, French, and British settled parts of the Caribbean and North America.

The way that Native Americans lived their lives greatly changed after they encountered the Europeans. The Spanish became known for their **encomienda system**, where they would enslave the Native Americans and force them to work the land, harvesting raw materials that the Spanish could sell for money. They also forced the Native Americans to convert to Christianity and abandon their own cultural traditions and languages. As soon as the Spanish realized that disease was killing too many Native Americans, they began to bring enslaved Africans to their colonies. Other European countries with colonies in the Americas also began to engage in the African slave trade. The slave trade was part of a larger trade network, known as the **Triangular Trade**. European colonies in the Americas sent raw materials like sugar, tobacco, cotton, and indigo, which had been harvested by slaves, back to Europe, where some of those materials would be made into goods like guns and textiles. Those goods would be sent to Africa and sold in exchange for enslaved Africans. Then those enslaved people would be sent to the Americas to harvest more raw materials.

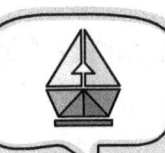
Triangular trade

NORTH
AMERICA

EUROPE

RAW MATERIALS

ATLANTIC
OCEAN

MANUFACTURED GOODS

13 COLONIES

CARIBBEAN ISLANDS

AFRICA

PACIFIC
OCEAN

ENSLAVED AFRICANS

SOUTH
AMERICA

1. Why did the Spanish enter into the slave trade?

....

....

....

2. What was sent from the colonies to Europe in the Triangular Trade?

....

....

3. Who was sent from Africa to the colonies in the Triangular Trade?

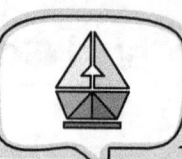
Directions: Read the text below. Then follow the instructions to complete the activity.

When the Native Americans first encountered Europeans, neither group had any idea what to expect. Neither group spoke each other's languages, so it was difficult to communicate. It was scary for the Native Americans as they were not sure what these foreigners wanted or if they were friendly. While relations could sometimes be positive between the Native Americans and the Europeans, there was often violence and mistrust. Considering both sides and perspectives, write a paragraph describing your feelings about the Europeans as if you were a Native American, and a paragraph describing your feelings about the Native Americans as if you were a European in the spaces below.

How I feel about the Europeans	How I feel about the Indigenous People

Directions: Read the text below. Then answer the questions that follow.

This week you have learned about European exploration and conquest of the Americas. Each voyage that the Europeans conducted was designed to gain valuable new information about the Americas, spread Christianity, find riches, conquer new lands, and bring glory to themselves and their country. The interactions between Europeans and Native Americans were oftentimes filled with violence that resulted in the destruction of many Native American civilizations. Using what you have learned this week, answer the questions below.

1. What reasons did the Native Americans have for being fearful of the Europeans?

....

....

....

2. Who benefited the most from the Triangular Trade? Why?

....

....

....

3. Do you think that disease, warfare, and slavery were inevitable in the Americas? What could the Europeans have done differently?

....

....

....

....

....

....

....

....

....

Exchange

The Columbian Exchange

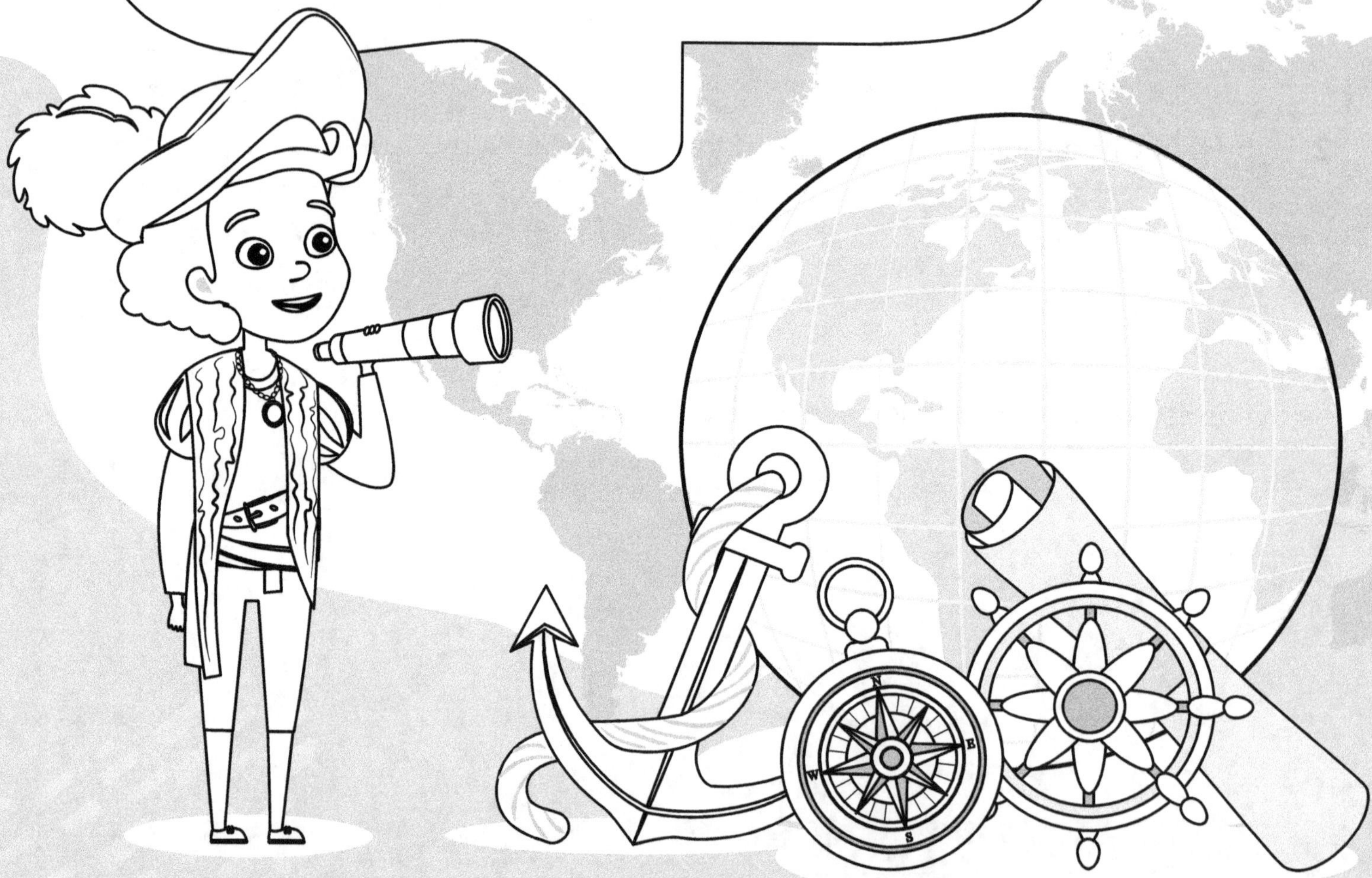

This week you will learn about the positive and negative results of trade between Europe and the Americas.

ARGOPREP

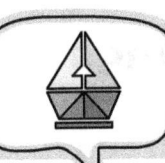
Directions: Read the text below. Then answer the questions that follow.

When European countries started exploring, conquering, and settling in the Americas, they brought with them a lot of plants and animals from Europe. They also encountered plants and animals that were native to the Americas, and brought those back to Europe. Over the course of several centuries of exploration, trade, and colonization, Europe and the Americas both gained many new plants and animals. This greatly changed the diets and agricultural techniques of everyone involved. Historians call this trading of plants and animals between Europe and the Americas the **Columbian Exchange**. Historians call it this because the first European to trade goods with Native Americans was Christopher Columbus. When Columbus first landed in the Caribbean, he remarked in his Captain's Log:

"They came swimming to the boats, bringing parrots, balls of cotton thread, javelins, and many other things, which they exchanged for the articles we gave them."

The Columbian exchange also included all of the cultural ideas, languages, religious beliefs, tools, and technologies that spread between Europe and the Americas. Unfortunately, not all of the exchanges between Europe and the Americas were friendly or fair. The Columbian Exchange also included the diseases brought to the Americas from Europe, as well as the trading of enslaved people.

1. What is the name of the exchange of goods and ideas between Europe and the Americas?

   A. The Northwest Exchange

   B. The Columbian Exchange

   C. The Silk Road

   D. The Western Migration

2. How did the exchange of plants and animals affect people in Europe and the Americas?

   A. It changed their culture.

   B. It changed their diet.

   C. It changed their religion.

   D. It changed their language.

3. Which of the following was not part of the Columbian Exchange?

   A. diseases

   B. religion

   C. war

   D. slavery

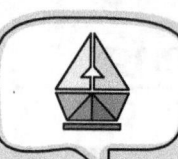
Directions: Examine the diagram below. Then answer the questions that follow.

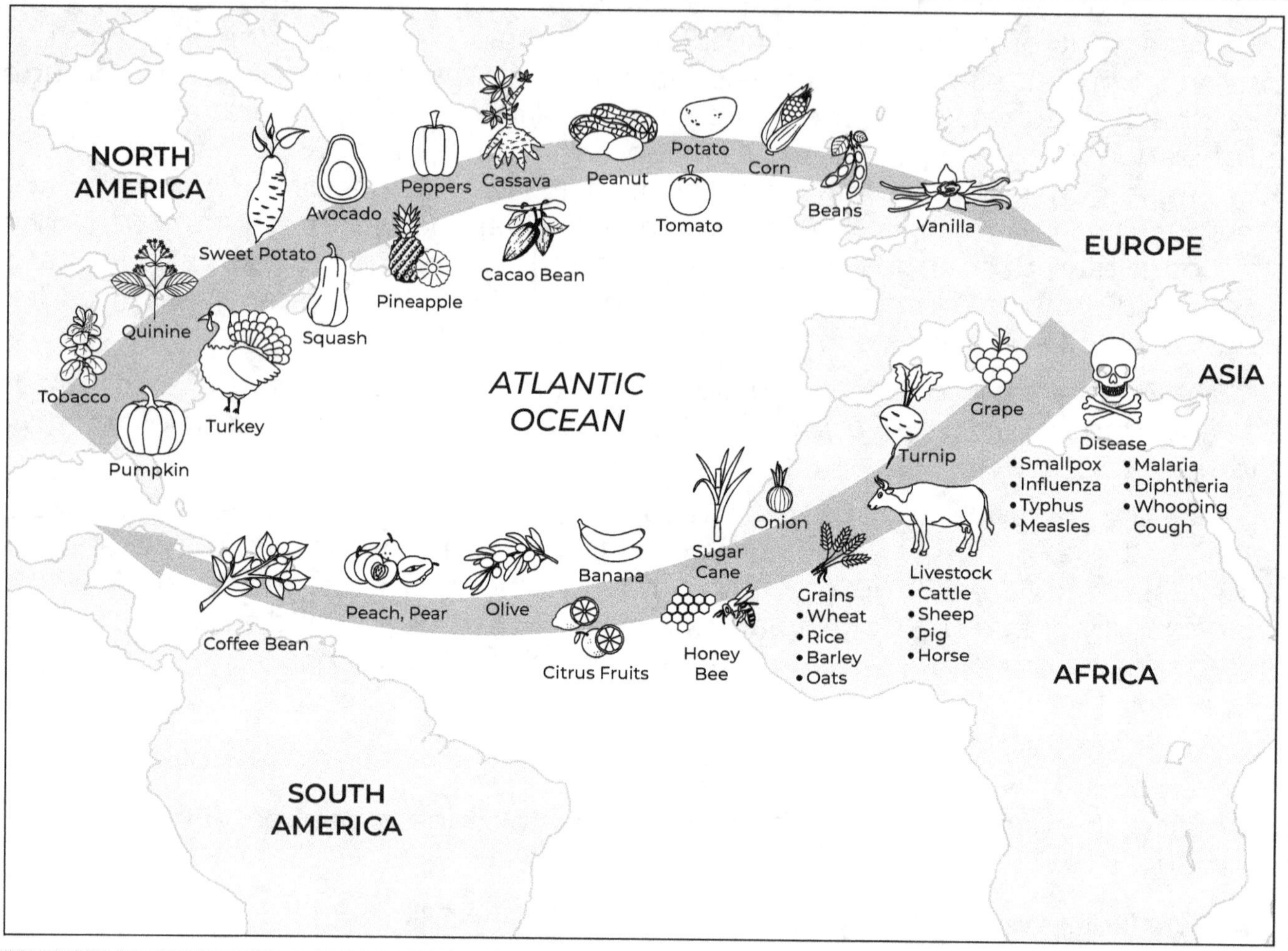

NORTH AMERICA

Avocado
Peppers
Cassava
Peanut
Potato
Corn
Sweet Potato
Beans
Tomato
Vanilla
EUROPE
Cacao Bean
Pineapple
Quinine
Squash
Tobacco
Turkey
Pumpkin

ATLANTIC OCEAN

Grape
ASIA
Turnip
Disease
• Smallpox   • Malaria
• Influenza • Diphtheria
• Typhus   • Whooping
• Measles   Cough

Onion
Banana
Sugar Cane
Peach, Pear
Olive
Coffee Bean
Citrus Fruits
Honey Bee
Grains
• Wheat
• Rice
• Barley
• Oats
Livestock
• Cattle
• Sheep
• Pig
• Horse
AFRICA

SOUTH AMERICA

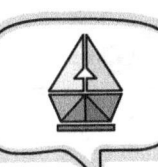
1. List three goods that were transported from the Americas to Europe.

....

....

....

....

2. List three goods that were transported from Europe to the Americas.

....

....

....

....

3. Research one of the diseases listed on the map and describe some of its negative side effects.

....

....

....

....

....

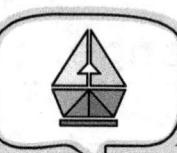
Directions: Read the text below. Then answer the questions that follow.

Some of the items traded between Europe and the Americas led to positive cultural changes for many Native Americans. One example of this is horses. Horses were brought to the Americas by the Spanish conquistadors. During their journeys, horses sometimes escaped. These horses traveled north toward the Great Plains, where Native Americans adopted them into their daily life. The introduction of the horse to Native American tribes of the Great Plains allowed them to hunt larger animals like bison, and to be more nomadic than they were before they had horses.

Other elements of the Columbian Exchange negatively impacted Native Americans and Africans. Sugar cane was brought to the Americas by Europeans. In the Caribbean, European settlers started large sugar plantations, where enslaved Native Americans and Africans would harvest the sugar cane. The European settlers were the ones who saw the benefit from the sugar trade, since they got to keep all of the profits from the labor of the enslaved people. The success of growing sugar cane and other **cash crops**, or crops that made the most money, such as tobacco, cotton, and indigo, was one of the main reasons for the continuation of the slave trade.

Europeans benefited greatly from the Columbian exchange, not just from the money made off of cash crops, but from the new foods introduced to Europe. After foods native to the Americas, such as maize, squash, beans, potatoes, and tomatoes were introduced to Europe, populations in Europe rose rapidly. Historians believe this happened because the foods in the Americas were extremely nutrient rich. When added to the foods Europeans already had, diets became more diverse, thus making everyone more healthy. Crops like potatoes were also easier to care for, less risky, and gave more food per acre than traditional European crops like wheat, rice, and barley. Meanwhile, the population of Native Americans plummeted, with nearly ninety percent of them dying from the diseases brought by Europeans.

1. How did the introduction of the horse impact the Native American tribes of the Great Plains?

....

....

....

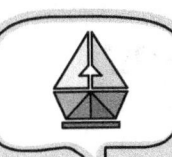
2. What do you think was the most impactful result of the Columbian Exchange? Explain your thinking.

....

....

....

3. Who do you think benefited the most from the Columbian Exchange, Native Americans or Europeans? Provide evidence and reasoning to support your claim.

....

....

....

....

....

....

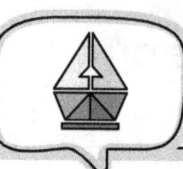
Directions: Read the text below. Then follow the instructions to complete the activity.

Imagine that you are engaging in the Columbian exchange as a European explorer, an enslaved African, or a Native American. As someone who would be experiencing the Columbian Exchange firsthand, describe what the effects of the exchange have been on your life. Make sure to describe the types of goods you have traded as well as received.

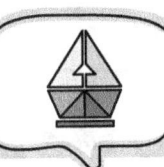
Directions: Read the text below. Then answer the questions that follow.

This week you have learned about the Columbian Exchange and its many positive and negative effects, as well as the many groups of people who were involved in it. Using this information, answer the questions below.

1. Which area of your life has been most impacted by the Columbian exchange? Explain your thinking.

....

....

....

....

2. Were the positive effects of the Columbian Exchange worth the negative consequences? Use evidence to support your reasoning.

....

....

....

....

....

....

....

....

....

....

WEEK 6

Exchange
The Middle Passage

This week you will learn about the economic system of slavery and the experiences of enslaved Africans during the Transatlantic Slave Trade.

ARGOPREP

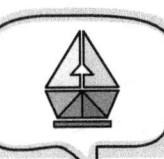
Directions: Read the text below. Then answer the questions that follow.

As European settlements in the Americas grew, wealthy European landowners in the Americas began creating **plantations**, or large-scale farms. Plantations were being created in the Caribbean and throughout the Americas to grow **cash crops**, or crops that make a lot of money. Sugarcane was the most important crop that was being grown on these large plantations in the Caribbean. In North America, most of the plantations grew tobacco or cotton. Plantation owners desired free labor in order to make as much money as possible. The solution to their greed was to purchase enslaved people to work on their farms for free.

You may recall the **Triangular Trade**, in which raw materials were sent from the Americas to Europe, and goods were sent from Europe to Africa. When Europeans began trading with Africa, one of their most desired resources was enslaved people. The part of the Triangular Trade in which enslaved people from Africa were sent on ships to the Americas is also known as the **Middle Passage**. European traders would trade various goods from Europe in exchange for enslaved people in West Africa, and then force them onto slave ships where they lived in cramped conditions that were unhygienic, inhumane, and deadly. The trip to the Americas took several months, and due to the cramped conditions, disease was rampant amongst the enslaved people, resulting in numerous deaths. Crew members recorded in log books that sharks would follow the slave boats waiting for the dead to be thrown overboard or for the enslaved to attempt to escape. The Middle Passage is known as the most horrific and deadly portion of the Triangular Trade between Europe, Africa, and the Americas. Yet for the enslaved people who were able to survive the voyage, a terrible fate awaited them, as they would endure a life of forced labor on plantations in the Americas.

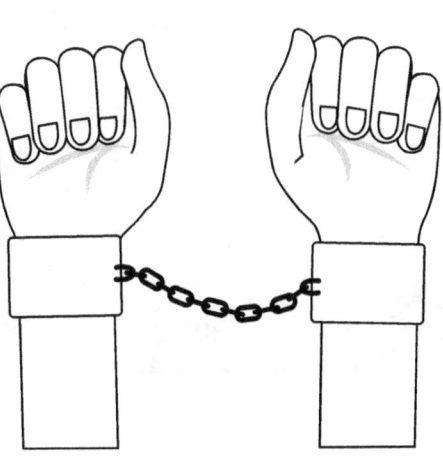

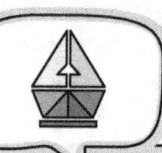
1. What was the most important crop grown on Caribbean plantations?

A. sugarcane

B. tobacco

C. rice

D. cotton

2. Why did plantation owners desire enslaved workers?

A. for affordable labor

B. for fair labor

C. for free labor

D. for expensive labor

3. What is the name for the portion of the Triangular Trade in which enslaved people from West Africa were brought to the Americas?

A. Sugar Trade

B. Plantation Route

C. Middle Passage

D. Columbian Exchange

4. Which portion of the triangular trade was the most deadly?

A. from Europe to the Americas

B. from the Americas to Europe

C. from Europe to Africa

D. from Africa to the Americas

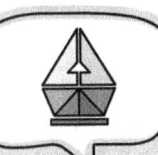
Directions: Read the text below. Then answer the questions that follow.

The Middle Passage exposed enslaved people to some of those most horrific aspects of humanity. They were packed into ships that were designed to carry far fewer people. They spent the entire journey in shackles below deck in the cargo hold and were only allowed to stand up and stretch for very short lengths of time. They were forced to sleep on stiff wooden planks and would have to go to the bathroom where they were lying. As one can imagine, the health of the enslaved people was incredibly poor, and many did not survive the Middle Passage. It is estimated that up to 2 million enslaved Africans died while being transported across the Middle Passage. Conditions were so poor that disease also claimed the lives of up to 20% of all crew members who were transporting the enslaved people. Examine the diagram below and answer the questions that follow.

A diagram of a slave ship

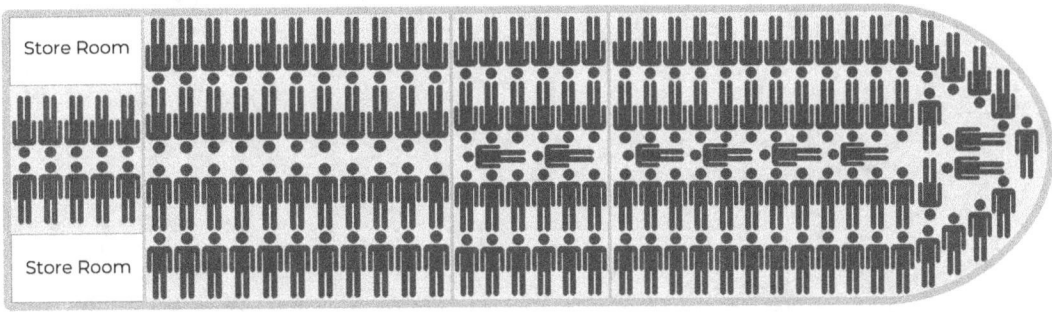

Plans of the lower cargo hold with the stowage of 292 enslaved people.

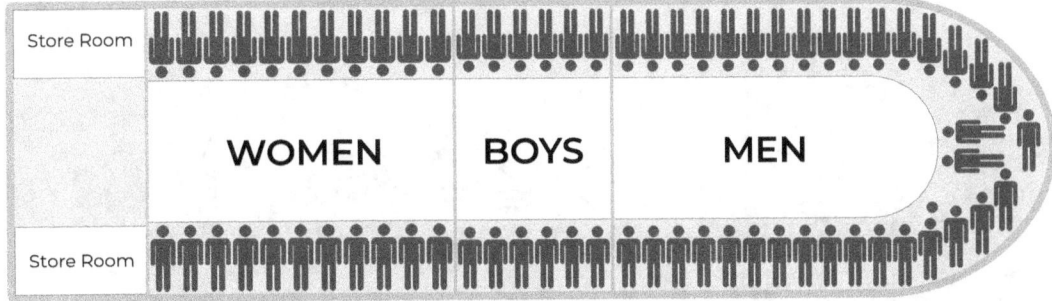

Plan showing the stowage of 130 of the 292 total enslaved people, stowed on platforms around the sides of the cargo hold. The people beneath these platforms had only 2 feet and 7 inches of space in which to lie down, and were unable to sit or stand.

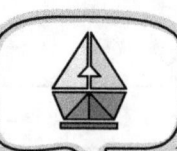
1. How many total enslaved people died on the Middle Passage?

....

2. List three of the most inhumane aspects of the Middle Passage for enslaved people:

A. ....

B. ....

C. ....

3. Why might slave ship captains have wanted to put as many enslaved people onto the ship as possible?

....

....

....

....

....

....

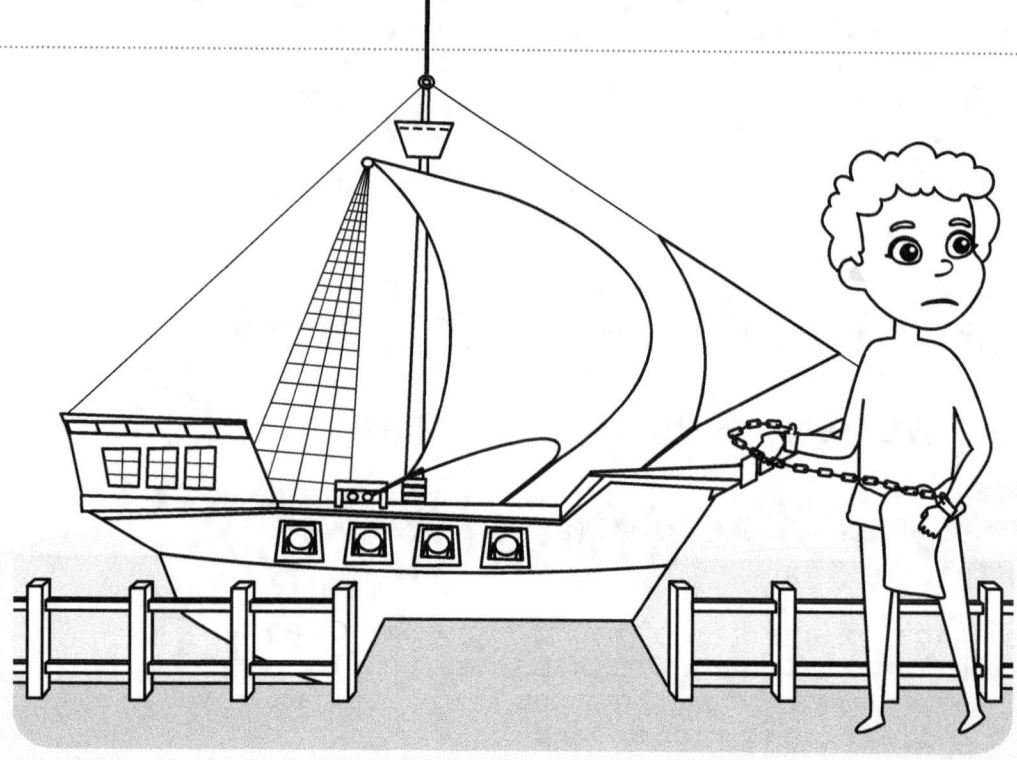

Directions: Read the text below. Then answer the questions that follow.

Packing a slave ship with human cargo became a science. Some captains believed that their ship was most efficient when it was as packed as possible, even if that meant a higher number of their enslaved cargo would die. Other captains believed that if they allowed more room for the enslaved people on their ships, they would minimize deaths and ultimately make more money. Such reasoning and thought processes regularly went through the minds of slave traders who were seeking large profits from selling their human cargo in the Americas.

The Middle Passage exposed the enslaved people on the ships to the most horrific conditions imaginable. They were forced to live in puddles of human waste with no fresh air, which caused the spread of many diseases. This led to a high number of deaths among the enslaved. Crew members would sometimes cut holes in the body of the ship to allow for air to flow through, but if there was heavy rain or otherwise poor weather, they would close these off and make the enslaved breathe the disease-ridden air.

The enslaved people were fed a minimal diet of foods such as corn, yams, and rice. There were often not enough provisions for the entire trip if there was poor weather that prolonged the journey. If food was short, only the crew ate and the enslaved people were forced to starve. Despite the horrible treatment, crew members did understand the need for the enslaved people to appear healthy so that they could sell them for the highest price possible. Once they landed in the Americas, they would cover the bodies of the enslaved people in oils and feed them well to make them appear healthy and strong in order to fetch the highest possible prices. The Middle Passage exposed the worst parts of humanity in that time period and is remembered as a horrific journey that millions of enslaved Africans were forced to endure on their way to living a life of slavery in the Americas.

1. Why did some slave ship captains arrange the enslaved people in less crowded conditions on their ships?

....

....

....

....

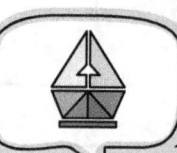
2. Given everything you have learned so far about the conditions on the slave ships, what do you believe the worst part of the journey would have been? Explain your reasoning.

....

....

....

3. Why might slave traders have been willing to make the journey across the Middle Passage multiple times despite the risk of disease?

....

....

4. Why did slave traders cover the enslaved people with oils and feed them well upon reaching the Americas?

....

....

....

Directions: Read the text below. Follow the instructions to complete the activity.

In your own words, describe what the Middle Passage was like for enslaved people. Use details from the readings to support your description.

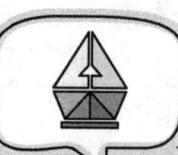
Directions: Read the text below. Follow the instructions to complete the activity.

Complete the cause and effect chart below using the information that you have learned this week.

Cause	Effect
European plantation owners in the Americas wanted free labor to make the most money possible off of their cash crops.	
	Hundreds of enslaved people were packed together in cargo holds of slave ships in unhygienic conditions with not enough food.
Hundreds of enslaved people were packed together in cargo holds of slave ships in unhygienic conditions with not enough food.	

WEEK 7

Geography

Geography of North America

This week you will learn about the different geographic regions of Canada, the United States, and Mexico.

ARGOPREP

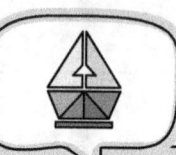
Directions: Read the text below. Then answer the questions that follow.

"

The landscape of North America is filled with a variety of breathtaking geographic features like the Rocky Mountains, the mountains of Appalachia, and the Grand Canyon, to name a few. From the cold **tundra** region in Canada, to the tropical and desert regions of Mexico, North America has a wide variety of different regions and climates.

Canada is the second largest country by landmass in the entire world. The United States is the third largest, with only Russia being larger than either. It has taken millions of years of development for North America to develop its unique geographic features, such as its roaring rivers, deep valleys, and towering mountain ranges. North America is home to some of the most diverse geography in the entire world. From the thousands of miles of untamed wilderness in Alaska and Canada, to the cities that make up what is called the **megalopolis** along the east coast of the United States, there is no shortage of diversity in both the natural and man-made wonders in North America.

"

1. The tundra is located in the .... in North America

   A. North   **B.** South   **C.** East   **D.** West

2. What is the largest Country in North America?

   A. Russia

   B. Canada

   C. The United States

   D. Mexico

3. Which country in North America has the warmest regions?

   A. Russia

   B. Canada

   C. The United States

   D. Mexico

4. A megalopolis is made up of ....

   A. mountains

   B. oceans

   C. glaciers

   D. cities

CANADA

USA

MEXICO

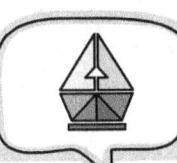
Directions: Read the text below. Then answer the questions that follow.

North America is home to numerous geographic regions that demonstrate the diverse offerings of climate, plant life, and natural formations of the continent.

The **Atlantic Coastal Plain** is a lowland region that runs across most of the eastern coast of the United States. In the northeast of this region, there is the megalopolis made up of cities like Boston, New York City, Washington, D.C., and Philadelphia, which all have important political and economic functions and serve as cultural centers of the country. The soil in these regions is rocky and thin, and farming is possible but only in certain areas, and with varying degrees of fertility. Instead, there is a large fishing industry, with numerous ports and harbors along the coast of the Atlantic Ocean.

The **Gulf Coastal Plain** is a lowland region near the Gulf of Mexico and includes states of Texas and Louisiana, Mississippi, Alabama, and Florida, as well as much of eastern Mexico. The soil tends to be very rich in this region and makes for great farming.

To the northwest of the Atlantic and Gulf Coast Plains are the **Appalachian Mountains**, which stretch from eastern Canada in the north all the way south to Alabama. The region around the Appalachian Mountains is called **Appalachia**. Many people live in this area and work in jobs related to the mountainous region around them, such as coal mining.

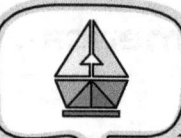
1. The Atlantic Coastal Plain is an example of a ....

    A. highland

    B. lowland

    C. tundra

    D. mountain

2. Why is it difficult to farm in the Atlantic Coastal Plain?

....

....

....

3. Match the industry with the region:

    .... Atlantic Coastal Plain   **A.** farming

    .... Gulf Coastal Plain   **B.** mining

    .... Appalachia   **C.** fishing

4. Which of the three regions discussed in the text is depicted in the image below?

....

Directions: Read the text below. Then answer the questions that follow.

The **tundra** region of northern Canada is noted for its extremely cold climate, as well as its limited plantlife and vegetation. The human populations in this region are also extremely low. Southern Canada is mostly part of the coniferous forest region. Common characteristics of the coniferous forest region include cold winters and cool summers, as well as vast forests of evergreen trees. Logging is one of the largest industries in this region.

Lakes and rivers serve many important roles for the people and ecosystems in the United States and Canada, including transportation and shipping. One of the largest and most important rivers in the United States is the Mississippi River, which includes the Missouri River, a **tributary**, or a river that flows into a larger river. The Mississippi River helps create very fertile land all across its length which makes the surrounding areas great for farming.

In the Northern United States there is the **Great Lakes** region. The Great Lakes include Lake Huron, Lake Ontario, Lake Michigan, Lake Erie, and Lake Superior, which were all created by the movement of glaciers over 10,000 years ago. The creation of man-made canals and **locks** allow ships to be raised and lowered from one lake into the other. Ships that begin on the St. Lawrence River to the northeast of the Great Lakes can travel through Canada all the way into the midwestern United States and back again because of these canals and locks. This means that goods and raw materials can be taken to and from big midwestern cities to all over the world through the waterways of the Great Lakes.

The country of Mexico is just as diverse in its geography as the United States and Canada. Mexico has high mountains, low valleys, dry deserts, tropical rainforests, and coastal plains. Overall, it has a warmer climate than the United States and Canada, since it is closer to the **equator**. However, there are places in Mexico in the high mountains that get some snow during part of the year. One of the largest industries in Mexico is mining, as the mountains contain vast mineral deposits.

1. Why do you think logging is one of the largest industries in Canada?

....

....

....

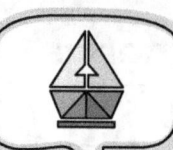
2. What are two benefits of the Mississippi River?

....

....

3. How do locks make the Great Lakes and St. Lawrence River easier for ships to travel?

....

....

4. Why does Mexico have a warmer climate than the United States and Canada?

....

....

....

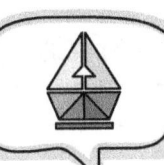
Directions: Read the text below. Then follow the instructions to complete the activity.

Every region in North America has unique features that separate it from other regions and from the rest of the world. The place where you live also has many geographic features that make it a unique area, and it is important to learn about some of these features. Using the internet and any other sources, look up the following information about the region that you live in.

Where do you live?

....

Do you live on a coastal plain, mountain region, or somewhere else?

....

What is the highest geographic point near you?

....

What is the largest body of water in your region?

....

What are three animals that are native to your region?

....

What are three types of plants that are native to your region?

....

Which big city are you closest to?

....

What is a popular industry near you?

....

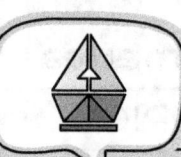
Directions: Read the text below. Then complete the activity that follows.

If you could live anywhere in North America where would it be? Why would you choose that place? What would life be like there? What type of job would you perform in the area that you chose? What might be some positives and negatives of living in that area?

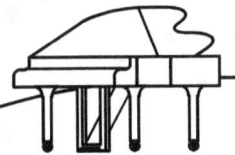

Individual Development

Immigration and Culture in the United States

This week you will learn about the many different cultures of the United States, a nation of immigrants.

ARGOPREP

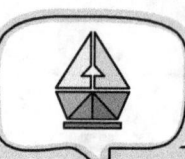
Directions: Read the text below. Then answer the questions that follow.

> The United States is a very unique country. It is home to a very diverse group of people who have come from many different places. We call these people **immigrants**. Everyone except for the Native Americans has either immigrated to America, or has descended from people who immigrated to America. The culture of the United States is very unique due to the presence of people from so many different countries. In many ways, these immigrants have successfully combined parts of their native cultures with the dominant cultures in the United States to form an all new, unique set of customs and traditions. Take a look at the graph below.

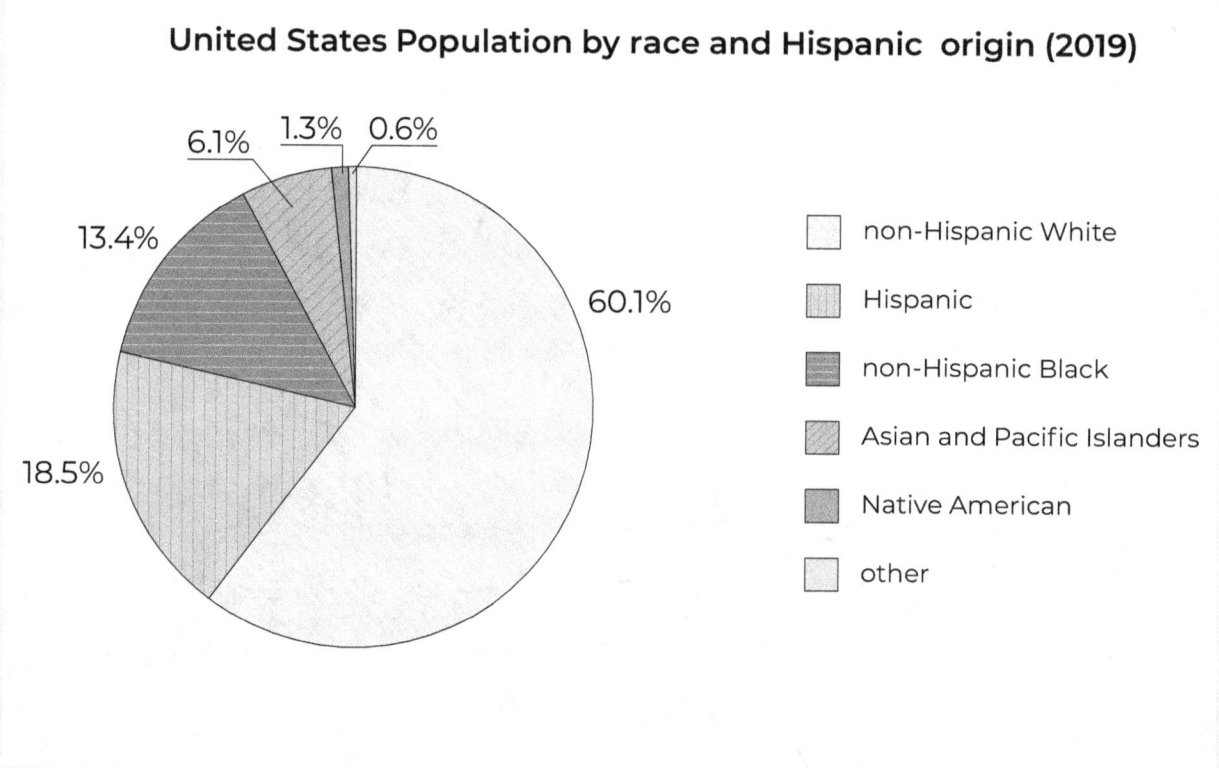

United States Population by race and Hispanic origin (2019)

- non-Hispanic White
- Hispanic
- non-Hispanic Black
- Asian and Pacific Islanders
- Native American
- other

> As you can see, there are many different groups that make up the United States population. When these people came to this country, they had no idea of what their futures held or what their lives would look like. They brought with them the **cultural traditions** and customs from their home countries. The United States is home to a wide variety of religions, the three most common being Christianity, Judaism, and Islam. It's not only religion that shows how diverse the United States is, but also

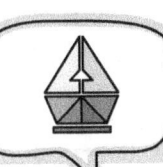
the many languages spoken in the country. English is the most common language, but unlike many other countries, the United States doesn't actually have an official language! The other most commonly spoken languages after English include Spanish, Mandarin, Tagalog, French, Vietnamese, German, Korean, and Russian.

The culture of the United States is different from any other in the world. With so many different groups of people having immigrated over the years, the blending of customs, traditions, languages, and religions have produced a distinct culture. This unique culture can be seen in the daily lives of people, the movies that are produced, the music that is listened to, and the books that are published. With so many people coming to the country consistently each year, the culture continues to evolve and change, but this consistent shift represents the diversity and strength of the entire nation.

1. The majority of the United States population is made up of ....

    A. Native Americans

    B. immigrants

    C. Non-Hispanic White people

    D. Hispanic people

2. What race is the second most common in the United States?

    A. Native American

    B. Hispanic

    C. Non-Hispanic White

    D. Non-Hispanic Black

3. Which of these is not among the three most common religions in the United States?

    A. Islam

    B. Christianity

    C. Buddhism

    D. Judaism

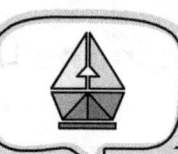
Directions: Read the text below. Then answer the questions that follow.

"

One of the best ways to learn about the culture of the United States is by reading different books, listening to many different varieties of music, and watching films.

Throughout the history of the United States, many authors like Frances Watkins Harper or Phillis Wheatley Peters have written about the unique experiences of different cultural groups. One of the most well-known authors in the country's history is Mark Twain. One of his most famous books, The Adventures of Tom Sawyer, gives a look into the lives of those who lived and worked along the Mississippi River in the 19th Century. Numerous other authors have written books that reflect their geographic regions and tell unique stories that all help paint a collective picture of United States life. During the Harlem Renaissance in the 1920's, poets like Langston Hughes wrote about the lives of African Americans.

Music has also been used as a method of personal and cultural expression in the United States. Think about all of the different genres of music that exist today. Country music represents a distinct lifestyle that first emerged in the early 20th century. Jazz emerged in the United States and blended existing marching band and orchestra elements with African beats and melody to create a distinct new genre of music. Rap, hip-hop, and rhythm and blues have all evolved from the earlier jazz and blues genres. The different cultural groups within the United States have all brought their own forms of music to the United States and these have blended together to create unique types of music that only exist in the United States.

Film presents a great opportunity to view life from the perspective of others. Various filmmakers have created works that have not only become popular across the United States but across the entire world. Whether it be a documentary which tells a real story about real people and situations or a musical telling a fictional love story or an adventure, film and television have become a staple of American culture ever since the 1950's. Various groups across the country have used film and television to tell stories of their unique cultures and their experiences in America.

"

1. What did Mark Twain write about?
   A. life in the American South
   B. life during the Harlem Renaissance
   C. life on the Mississippi River
   D. life in the 1950s

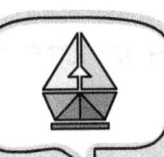
2. What group of people did Langston Hughes write about?

    A. Native Americans   **C.** Asian Americans

    B. African Americans   **D.** Italian Americans

3. What type of music emerged by blending existing elements of orchestra music with African beats and melody?

    A. country   **C.** rhythm and blues

    B. hip-hop   **D.** jazz

4. When did film and television become a large part of American culture?

    A. 1890s

    B. 1920s

    C. 1950s

    D. 1980s

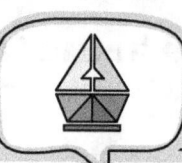
Directions: Read the text below. Then answer the questions that follow.

"

One reason why the United States has developed such a unique culture is because it has allowed immigrants to come into the country for hundreds of years. In fact, the nation was founded by immigrants. People have been coming to the United States for a variety of reasons ever since the first colonies were founded over 400 years ago. Many people from Europe came to escape religious persecution, famine, war, or poverty in their home countries. For example, the Irish brought their unique culture and traditions to the United States throughout the mid-1800s as they sought to escape a horrible potato famine that began in 1845. By 1850, more than 500,000 Irish had come to the United States and began to settle in various areas, mainly across the northeast. Other people did not come to America by choice. In 1619, the first enslaved Africans were brought to America against their will. Over 10 million enslaved Africans came to America between 1619 and 1808. However, they would not gain freedom for another 57 years. The culture of enslaved Africans had a profound impact on American culture, including their foods and musical traditions.

Out west, the discovery of gold in California would draw not just Americans but Chinese immigrants who were searching for the precious metal. After nearly 30,000 immigrants came over from China within two years, the U.S. government banned Chinese immigrants from the country. However, they continued to allow immigrants from Europe to come. By 1892, there were so many immigrants coming into the country that a processing center called Ellis Island was opened in New York City. Over 12 million European immigrants would enter the United States through Ellis Island from various parts of Europe over the next half century. Most recently, the United States has been receiving most of their new immigrants from Latin America and Asia, with a small percentage coming from Europe. Upon settling into their new lives in the United States, these immigrants have introduced aspects of their culture, adding to an already diverse country.

"

1. What are two reasons why people came to America in the past?

....

....

....

....

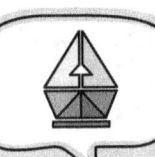
2. Which group came to the United States due to a famine in their country?

   A. Italians

   B. Chinese

   C. Irish

   D. Africans

3. Which group came to the United States against their will?

   A. Italians

   B. Chinese

   C. Irish

   D. Africans

4. Do you think that it was fair for the United States to ban the immigration of Chinese people while still allowing millions of European immigrants into the country? Use evidence from the reading to support your answer.

....

....

....

....

....

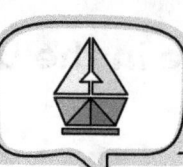
Directions: Read the text below. Then follow the instructions to complete the activity.

Consider your own family's history. Where did your family live before coming to the United States? Ask someone at home where your ancestors came from if you do not know, and then research some of the features of that culture and fill in the information below as if you are a new immigrant coming into the United States.

What is my name?

....

Where am I from?

....

What language(s) do I speak?

....

What are my favorite foods?

....

What is my favorite sport?

....

What is my favorite hobby?

....

What type of job would I like to have?

....

What are three things people may not know about my culture?

....

Directions: Read the text below. Then follow the instructions to complete the activity.

Imagine you have just immigrated to the United States. Where have you immigrated from? Why did you leave your home country? What would be some of the most difficult parts of coming to a new country? Do people accept you? Which aspects of your culture do you hope to maintain during your new life here? Which aspects of your culture are you afraid of losing? Is life here better than your home country? Write a letter to your family back in your home country in the space below.

WEEK 9

Individual Development

Canadian Culture

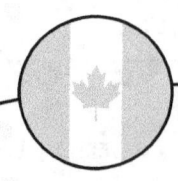

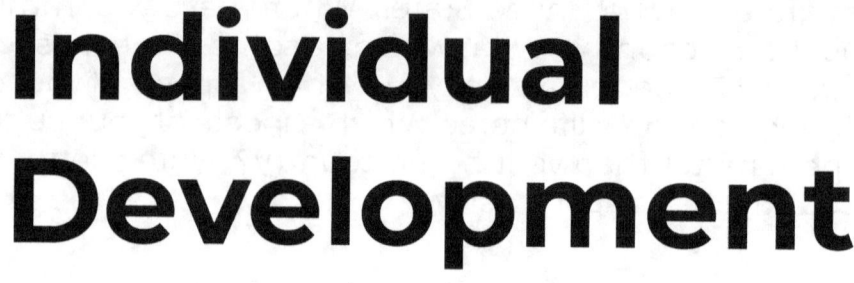

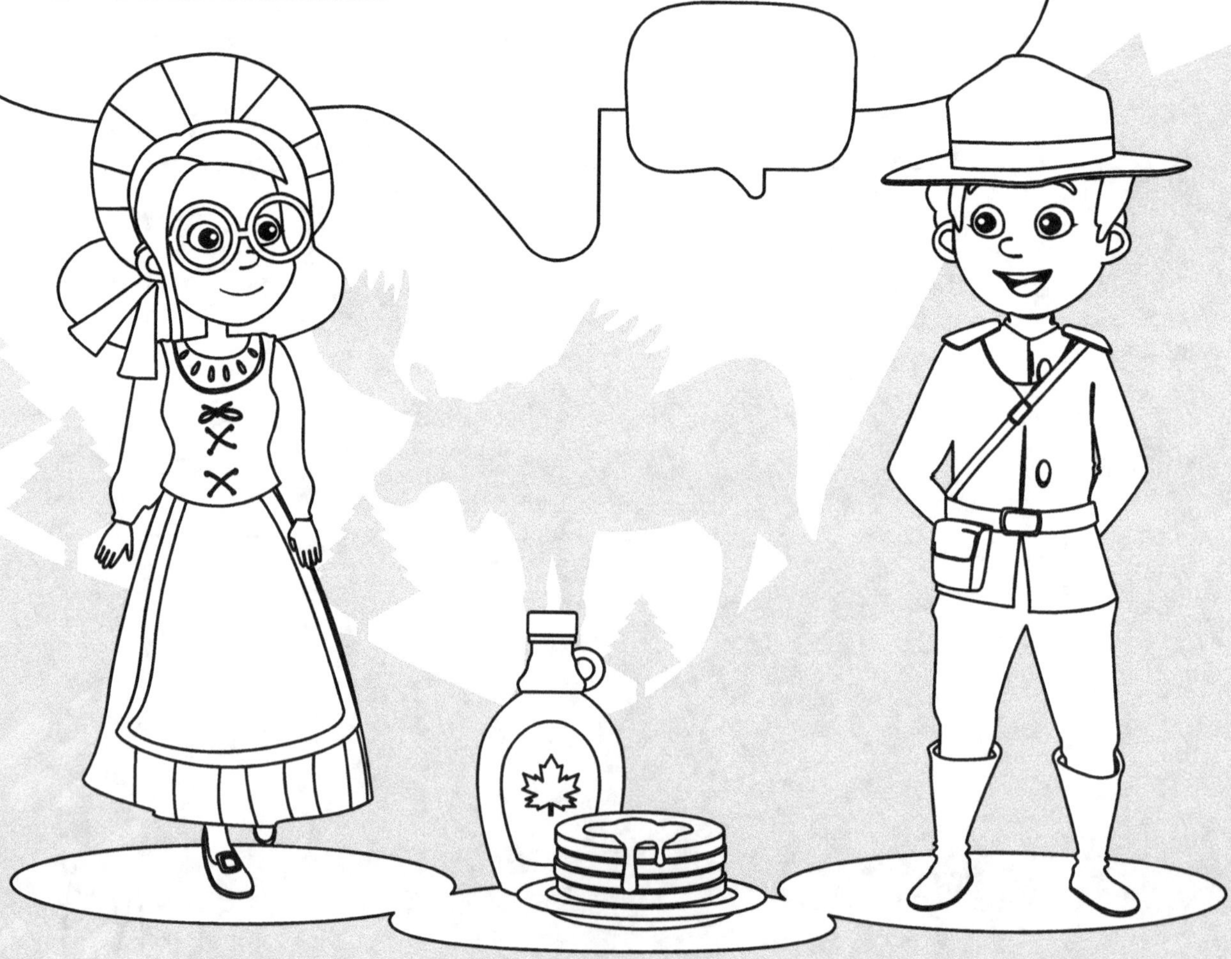

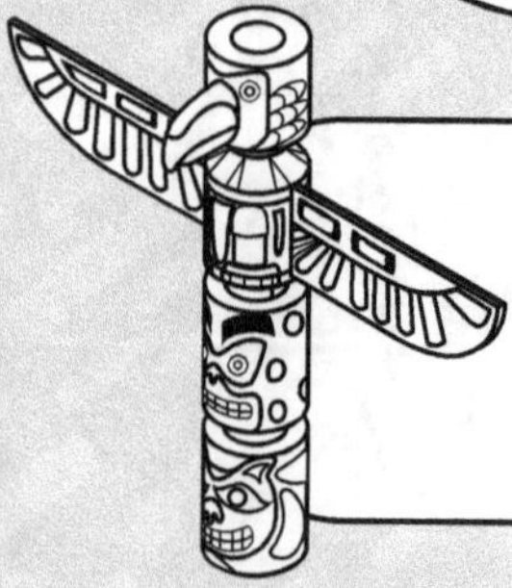

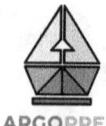

This week you will learn about the culture of Canada and compare it to what you have learned about the culture of the United States.

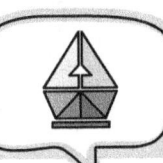
Directions: Read the text below. Then answer the questions that follow.

"

Canada has had a mix of cultures present within its boundaries for hundreds of years. First settled by the French in the 1600s and later taken over by the British after the French and Indian War, Canada has been exposed to a variety of cultures and customs. Canada is called a **bilingual** nation, meaning it has two official languages: French and English. Canada is home to people from all over the world who celebrate different holidays, enjoy different foods, and follow many different religions. With over thirty million citizens, Canada is home to many immigrants who have moved from various places around the world into the country. There are also millions of Indigenous Peoples, also referred to as First Peoples, who still continue to live in Canada. Many Indigenous People live on **reservations**, which is land the Canadian government set aside for them after most of their land was taken by European settlers. The United States and Canada are very similar in regard to culture and government. Due to these similarities, the countries have a good relationship with one another.

"

1. Which European country first settled in Canada?

   A. Britain

   B. The Netherlands

   C. France

   D. Germany

2. A bilingual nation has how many official languages?

   A. one

   B. two

   C. three

   D. four

3. Who lives on reservations in Canada?

   A. French

   B. English

   C. Indigenous Peoples

   D. Americans

4. What word best describes the relationship between the United States and Canada?

   A. positive

   B. neutral

   C. negative

   D. hateful

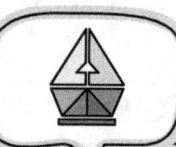
Directions: Read the text below. Then answer the questions that follow.

Canada is home to many cultures and people. Just like the United States, Canada welcomes immigrants from all over the world, and together they form a unique culture that is a blend of all of these groups together. Examine the map below to learn about the different languages spoken in Canada.

Languages spoken by the majority in Canada

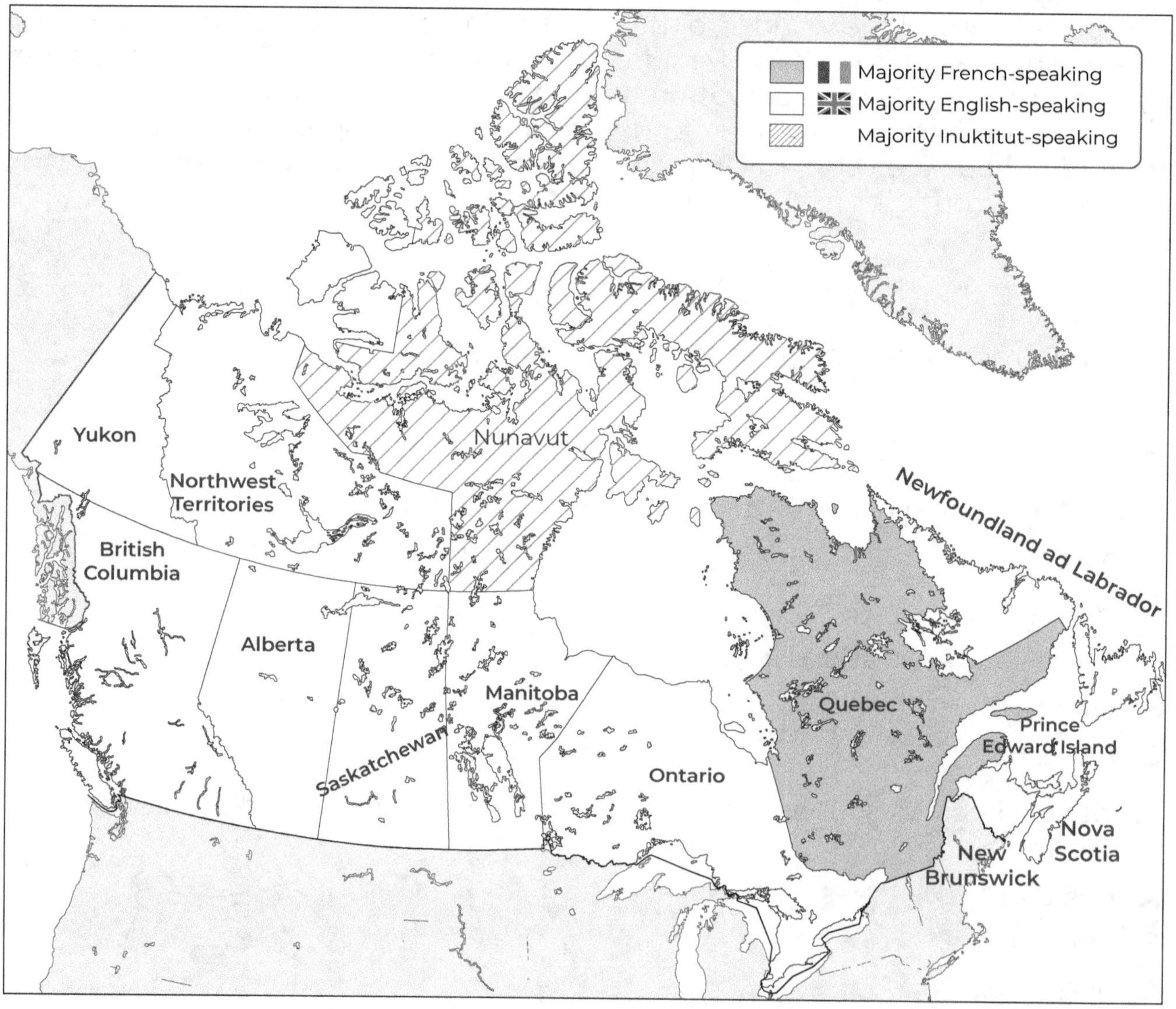

▓ ▌▌	Majority French-speaking
☐ ⊞	Majority English-speaking
▨	Majority Inuktitut-speaking

Yukon

Northwest Territories

British Columbia

Alberta

Saskatchewan

Manitoba

Nunavut

Ontario

Quebec

Newfoundland ad Labrador

Prince Edward Island

Nova Scotia

New Brunswick

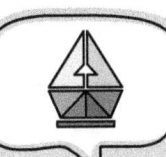
1. Which region of Canada mainly speaks French?

....

2. Why do you think there are two official languages in Canada?

....

....

3. The third most common language of Canada is Inukitut. Who do you think speaks this language?

....

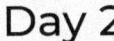

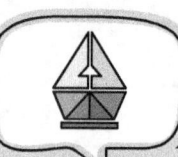
Directions: Read the text below. Then answer the questions that follow.

Canada is home to many diverse people who live within areas that are called **provinces**. Much like the states in the United States, provinces are areas that have their own government that makes laws and regulations but also obeys the laws set by the national Canadian government. While most Canadians truly love the country they live in, many people feel that they do not have much in common with other Canadians since the country is so large, and rather relate to people in their province. The province of Nunavut is the largest out of all Canadian provinces. In 1999, the province of Nunavut was created by taking part of the Northwest Territory province and giving it back to the Inuit, its native people. The Inuit demanded that their land be returned to them. The Inuit people traditionally survived through fishing and hunting but have taken to more modern techniques for making their living. For example, the Inuit people use snowmobiles for transportation in the cold and snowy region of Nunavut.

Canadian music is very similar to the music that people in the United States enjoy. Two of the biggest international music stars from the last decade have been Canadians - Justin Bieber and Drake. Historically, Irish and Scottish music grew in popularity in Canada starting in the 1700s. Many movies and actors that are world renowned are also from Canada. Even the United States films many of its films in Canada each year, mainly in big cities like Vancouver to the west and Toronto in the East.

With a prominent immigrant population, Canada boasts many different food options. Eastern European commodities and Italian foods are common across the Eastern portion of the country, while French food is very common in Quebec. Out west, more seafood and Asian foods are commonly enjoyed. Just like the United States, all of these people have been able to bring their unique culture to Canada and help create a vibrant immigrant community across the nation.

1. What are the different areas of government called in Canada?

   A. territories

   B. provinces

   C. neighborhoods

   D. commonwealths

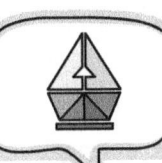
2. Which province is the largest in Canada?

....

3. What are the native people of Canada commonly called?

....

4. Why might Asian cuisine be more popular on the West Coast of Canada?

....

....

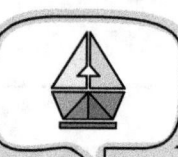
Directions: Read the text below. Then answer the questions that follow.

Many different groups have expressed the desire to be independent from the rest of Canada throughout the country's history. While the Inuit succeeded in their attempts, many other groups still wish to separate from Canada as well.

1. Why might a group of people want to become independent from the rest of their country?

....

....

....

2. Should a group of people or province be allowed to become independent? List three benefits and three drawbacks for allowing groups to become independent.

....

....

....

....

....

....

3. How could a group convince their country that they should be independent without going to war?

....

....

....

....

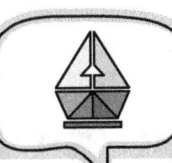
Directions: Read the text below. Then follow the instructions to complete the activity.

This week you have learned about Canadian culture. Last week, you learned about culture in the United States. Using what you have learned, fill in the Venn Diagram below.

Canada   United States

WEEK 10

Individual Development

Latin American Culture

This week you will learn about Latin American culture and how it compares to the culture of Canada and the United States.

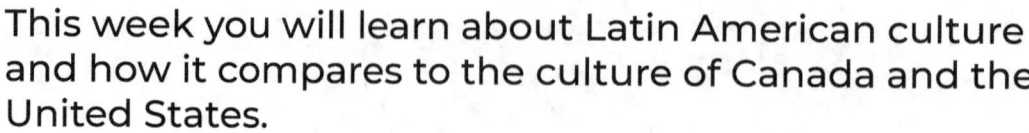

ARGOPREP

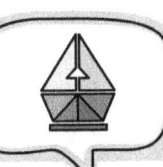
Directions: Read the text below. Then answer the questions that follow.

Latin America includes Central and South America, and is known for its unique culture, arts, literature, music, and overall way of life. There are considerable differences between the culture of the United States and Canada and the culture of Latin America. Religion is a focal point of Latin American culture, and the most widespread of all religions is Catholic Christianity. Although this is the most common religion for Latin Americans, there are significant groups of Muslims, Hindus, and other East Asian religions as well. Family is another very important aspect of Latin American culture. It is not uncommon for grandparents to live in a home with their children and grandchildren, and for adult siblings to live near each other as neighbors or even in the same house. Holidays are an extremely important part of Latin American life, too, the same way they are in the United States and Canada. There are some common holidays that are shared by all three cultures, including Columbus day, which is called Día de la Raza, or the Day of the Race, in Latin America. One holiday that is unique to Latin America is el Día de los Muertos, or The Day of the Dead. It is one of the largest celebrations throughout Latin America, as people in this culture believe that death is the beginning of a new phase of life and should be celebrated.

1. Latin America includes _____.
   - **A.** North, Central, and South America
   - **B.** Central and South America
   - **C.** North and South America
   - **D.** North and Central America

2. Grandparents often live with their children and grandchildren in Latin America. This shows the cultural importance of _____.
   - **A.** religion
   - **B.** work
   - **C.** family
   - **D.** school

3. What is the dominant religion in Latin America?
   - **A.** Hinduism
   - **B.** Buddhism
   - **C.** Catholic Christianity
   - **D.** Judaism

4. Which holiday is based around the belief that death is the beginning of a new phase of life?
   - **A.** Cinco de Mayo
   - **B.** Día de los Muertos
   - **C.** Día de la Raza
   - **D.** Columbus Day

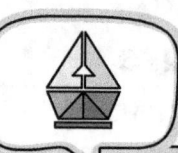
Directions: Read the text below. Then answer the questions that follow.

While baseball is known as "America's Pastime," and hockey is the most popular sport played in Canada, **fútbol**, commonly called soccer in the United States, is the most popular and widely played sport in all of Latin America. The sport is played by most children and adults and is one of the oldest sports (an early variation of this sport was played by the Maya and Aztec) in the entire world. Soccer is considered a communal activity, where neighbors, family members, and other members of the community routinely get together to play the game they all know and love. In recent years, other sports have become more popular in Latin America, too, and some are even more popular than soccer, depending on what part of Latin America you are from.

Percentage of Latin American Children Who Enjoy Various Sports

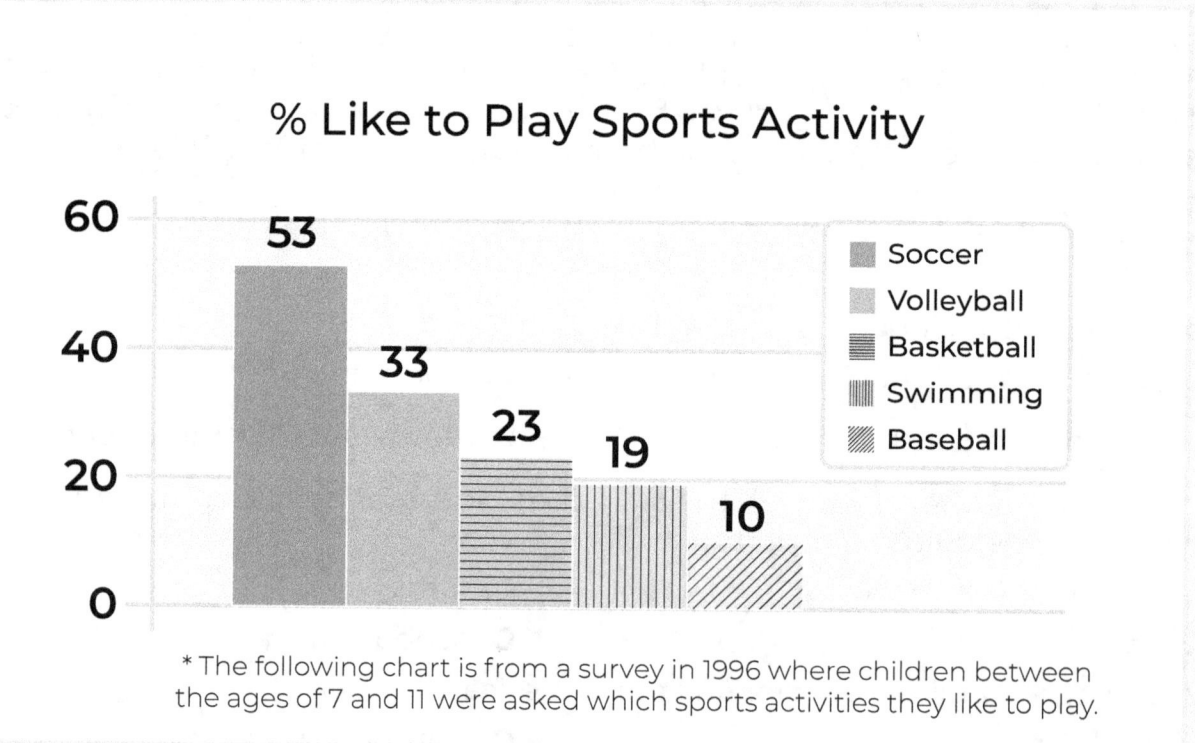

% Like to Play Sports Activity

Legend:
- Soccer
- Volleyball
- Basketball
- Swimming
- Baseball

Values: 53, 33, 23, 19, 10

* The following chart is from a survey in 1996 where children between the ages of 7 and 11 were asked which sports activities they like to play.

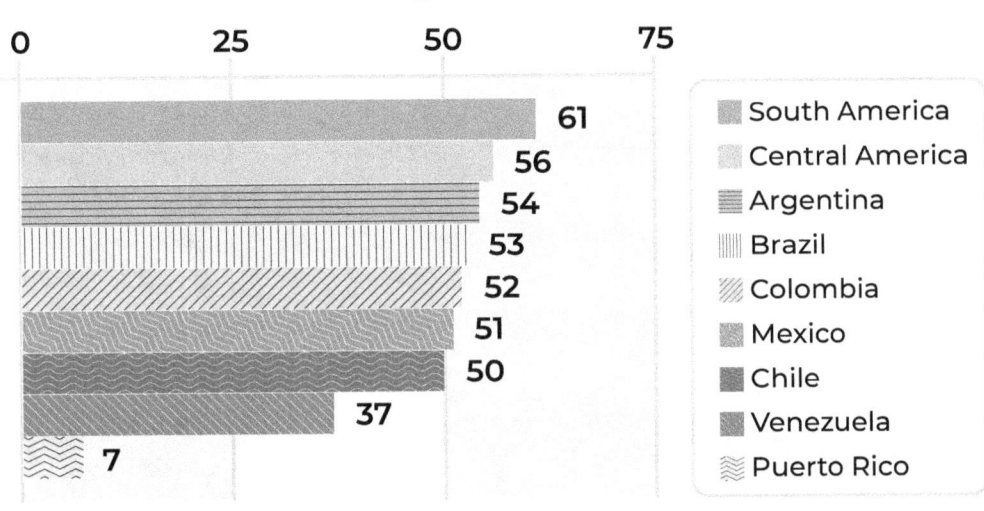

% Like to Play Soccer by Region

Region	%
South America	61
Central America	56
Argentina	54
Brazil	53
Colombia	52
Mexico	51
Chile	50
Venezuela	37
Puerto Rico	7

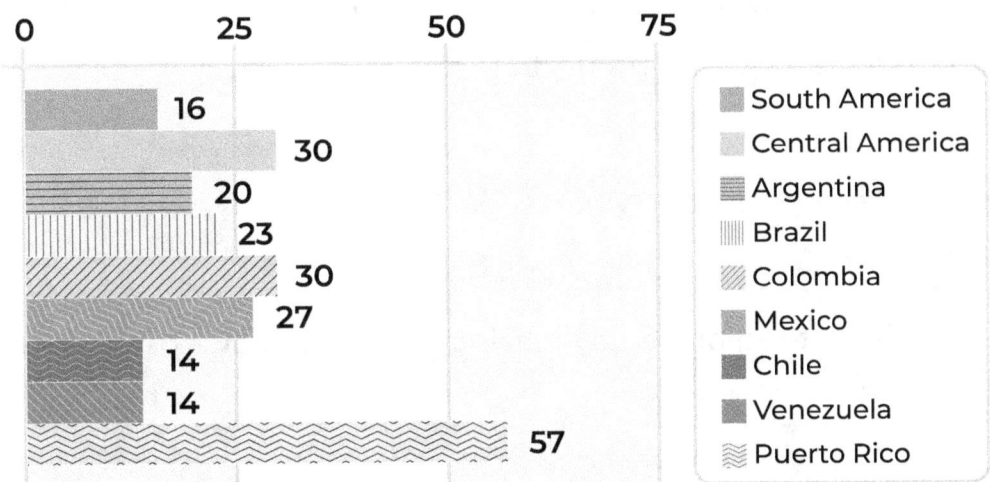

% Like to Play Basketball by Region

Region	%
South America	16
Central America	30
Argentina	20
Brazil	23
Colombia	30
Mexico	27
Chile	14
Venezuela	14
Puerto Rico	57

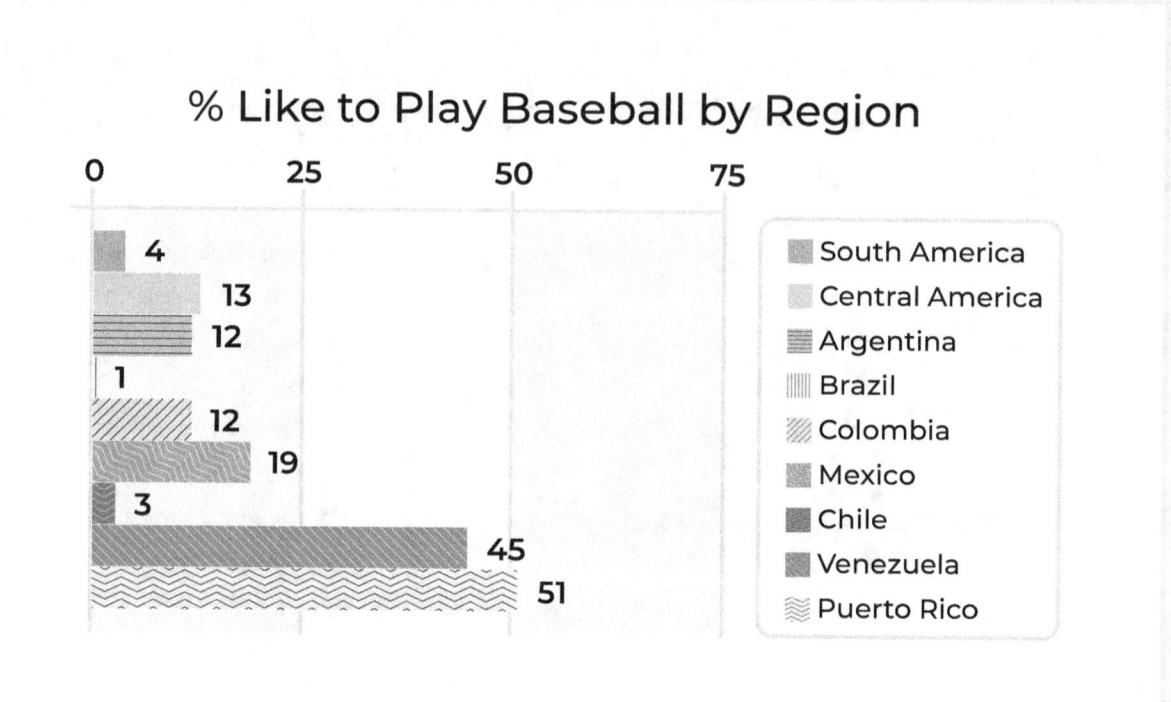

% Like to Play Baseball by Region

Legend:
- South America
- Central America
- Argentina
- Brazil
- Colombia
- Mexico
- Chile
- Venezuela
- Puerto Rico

Values: 4, 13, 12, 1, 12, 19, 3, 45, 51

1. Which sport is most popular in Latin America?

A. soccer　　　**B.** basketball　　　**C.** baseball　　　**D.** volleyball

2. Which sport is most popular in Puerto Rico?

....

3. Which sport is least popular in Puerto Rico?

....

4. Why might different regions enjoy playing different sports than other regions?

....
....
....
....

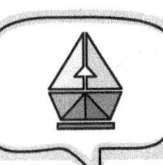
Directions: Read the text below. Then answer the questions that follow

El Día de los Muertos, or the Day of the Dead, is a commonly celebrated holiday throughout Latin America. The holiday commemorates the lives of loved ones who have died. The celebration is characterized by its food, drink, and overall festive nature, as celebrators welcome their deceased relatives back to Earth for a short reunion. The holiday coincides with Halloween, on October 31st, and lasts until November 2nd. Each individual day has its own specific name, with the 31st being Halloween, the 1st being el Día de los Inocentes, the Day of the Children, and the 2nd being el Día de los Muertos. It is believed that the origins of the Day of the Dead go back to the Aztec, who saw death as an ever present part of life, and used skulls as symbols to celebrate the dead. In ancient Aztec culture, it was believed that the dead went through a journey for several years before reaching their final resting place, called Mictlan. These indigenous beliefs blended with the Catholic celebrations when Europeans came to Central and South America, introducing All Saints Day on November 1st and All Souls Day on November 2nd. In many regions, this part of the year also marks the end of the harvest season. People gradually adopted the practice of leaving food and drink out on altars or on their loved one's graves to symbolize their offerings in helping them reach the end of their journey. Common symbols associated with the Day of the Dead are skeletons and skulls. Children and adults wear skull masks and eat skull shaped candies as well as spicy dark chocolates. The holiday has become a commercial event, too, with many films and pop culture references made about the celebrations. Mexico City held its first Day of the Dead parade in 2016, and shortly after many United States cities with strong Latin American communities held their own, too. Although the holiday has changed over the years in regard to how it is celebrated, the underlying meaning has always been the same. The remembrance of those who have passed on to the next life and the acknowledgement that they are still here with us is why millions of people continue to celebrate every year.

1. Where did el Día de los Muertos originate?

....

2. What US holiday does the first day of the Day of Dead coincide with?

....

3. What are two symbols commonly associated with the Day of the Dead?

....

4. Do you think that celebrations will continue to grow across North America in the next few years? Why or why not?

....

....

....

....

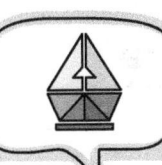
Directions: Read the text below. Then follow the instructions to complete the activity.

It is common for children to make their own skull masks for the Day of the Dead holiday throughout Latin America. Using the template below, draw your skull mask and color it with any colors you choose and include any designs to make it unique!

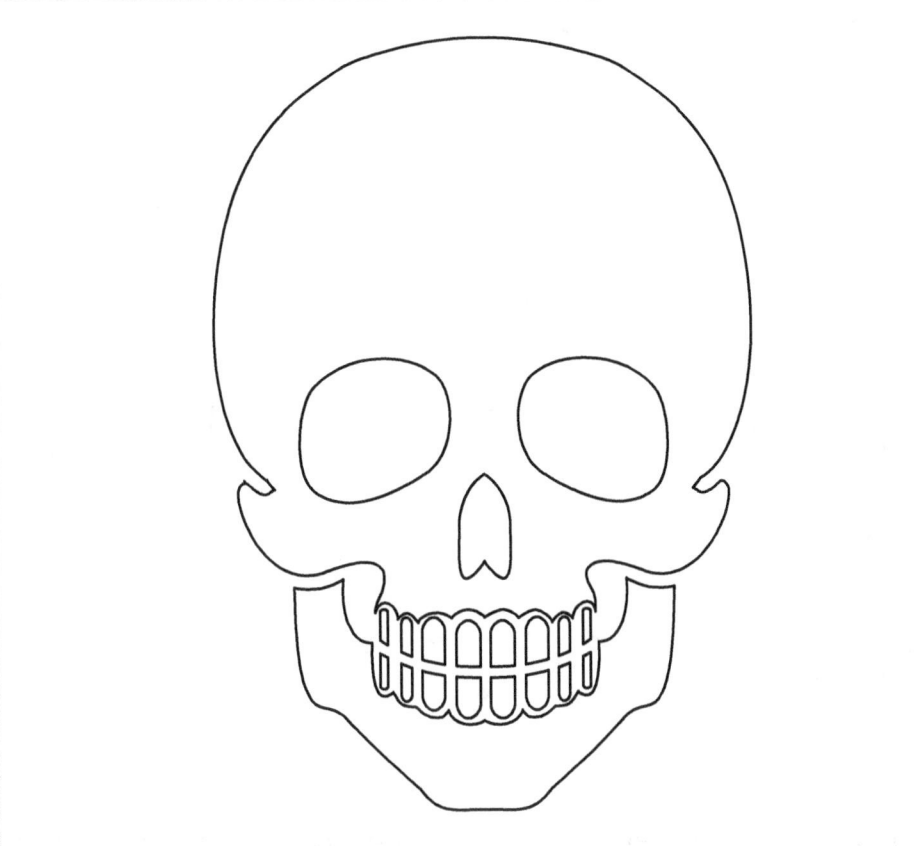

1. Who would your family be celebrating on el Día de Los Muertos?

....

....

2. Many people create 'ofrendas,' or a special place where they put up images of deceased family members and friends. They also put out reminders of that person's favorite things, such as a type of food or drink. What would you put on an *ofrenda* for the person you wrote about in #1?

....

....

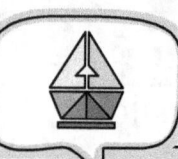
Directions: Read the text below. Then answer the questions that follow.

This week you learned about Latin American culture. In previous weeks you have learned about the culture of the United States and Canada.

1. What is one similarity between Latin American culture and North American culture? Why do you think both regions share this cultural characteristic?

....

....

....

....

2. Why do you think sports are so important across both Latin American and North American cultures?

....

....

....

....

3. How might el Día de los Muertos be perceived by someone outside of Latin America? What might someone assume about the holiday if they knew nothing about it other than what they saw in pictures?

....

....

....

....

....

....

WEEK 11

Geography

Environmental Issues in the Western Hemisphere

This week you will learn how climate change and environmental disasters affect the lives of citizens in the Western Hemisphere.

ARGOPREP

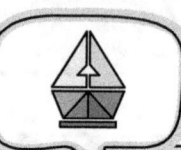
Directions: Read the text below. Then answer the questions that follow.

> The world is currently facing environmental challenges that we must work together to solve. In the United States, Canada, and Latin America, there can be any number of natural disasters that wreak havoc on human lives and communities. Common examples of these environmental issues include hurricanes, floods, and tornadoes. Scientists have learned **greenhouse gasses**, like carbon dioxide, that come from factories and other human activities get trapped in the atmosphere. They have also found that an increase of greenhouse gasses in the atmosphere are trapping heat, which is causing **global warming**. Global warming affects weather patterns, which has resulted in an increase of natural disasters such as tornadoes and hurricanes. The countries in the Western Hemisphere, particularly those in North America, have a big role to play in preventing and reversing environmental issues. Countries must all work together to minimize their impact on global warming. Doing so will prevent more natural disasters from harming their citizens and destroying their communities.

1. Which of the following is not a natural disaster?

   A. flood

   B. hurricane

   C. war

   D. tornado

2. Which of the following is a greenhouse gas?

   A. carbon dioxide

   B. oxygen

   C. helium

   D. none of the above

3. What is the cause of global warming?

   A. natural disasters

   B. greenhouse gasses

   C. weather patterns

   D. climate change

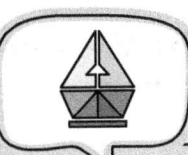

4. Who is affected the most by climate-related disasters?

    A. the Western Hemisphere

    B. governments and leaders

    C. factories and industries

    D. citizens and communities

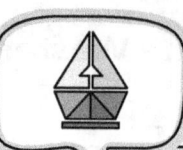
Directions: Read the text below. Then answer the questions that follow.

A **hurricane** is a storm that starts and gains strength in the ocean. Hurricanes usually develop over warm water. As the oceans warm, the number of hurricanes has increased. Hurricanes that make it to land cause destruction and death. The high waves and raging winds flood entire cities and destroy homes, schools, and business. Most hurricanes in North America make landfall in the southeastern United States, along the Gulf of Mexico. Hurricane Katrina was one of the most destructive hurricanes in the history of the United States. In 2005, the storm killed nearly 2,000 people and inflicted massive amounts of damage. The chart below details some of the most severe hurricanes in North America in recent history.

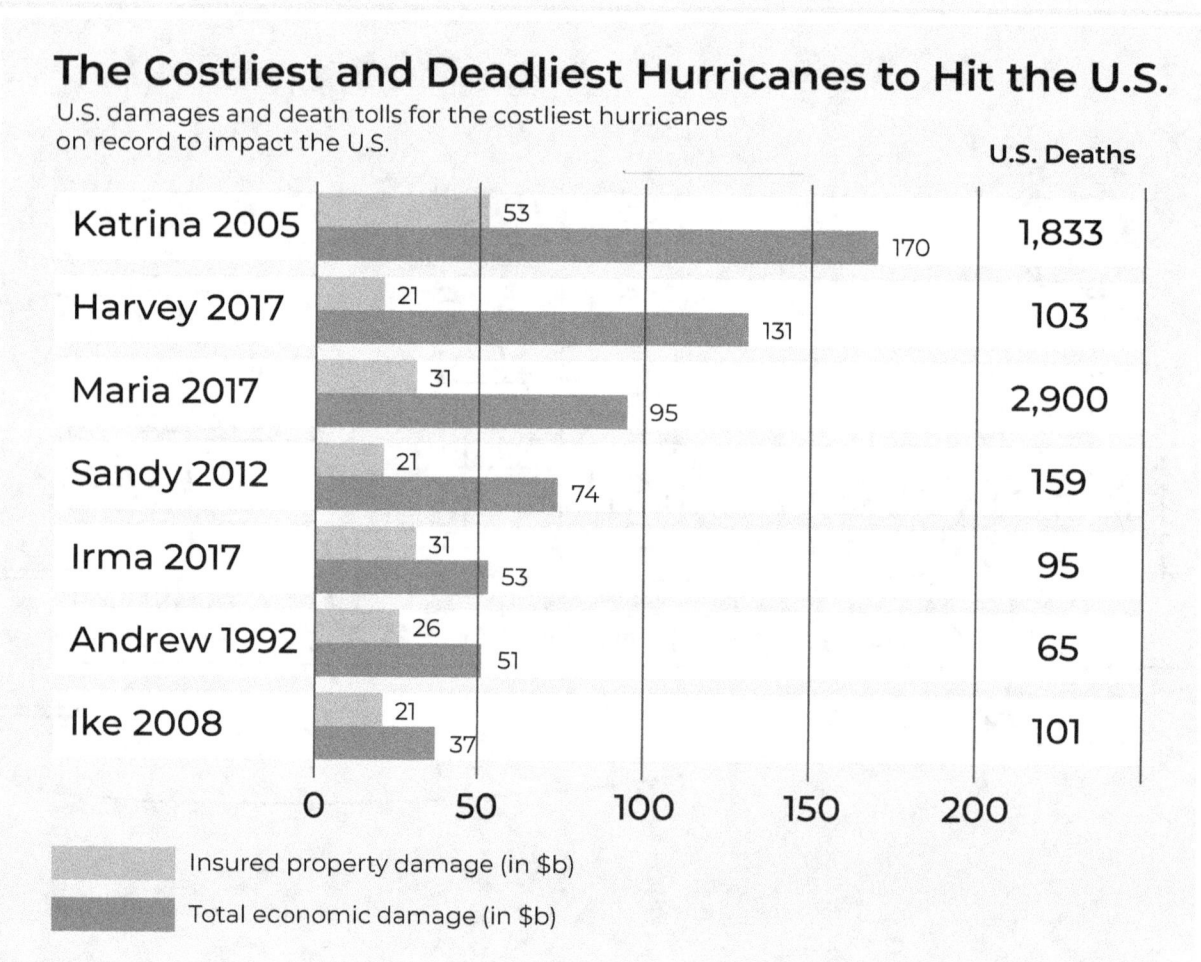

The Costliest and Deadliest Hurricanes to Hit the U.S.

U.S. damages and death tolls for the costliest hurricanes on record to impact the U.S.

Hurricane	Insured property damage (in $b)	Total economic damage (in $b)	U.S. Deaths
Katrina 2005	53	170	1,833
Harvey 2017	21	131	103
Maria 2017	31	95	2,900
Sandy 2012	21	74	159
Irma 2017	31	53	95
Andrew 1992	26	51	65
Ike 2008	21	37	101

Insured property damage (in $b)

Total economic damage (in $b)

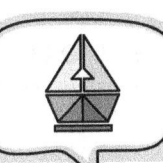
1. What type of climate causes hurricanes?

....

2. What is the result of a hurricane that hits land?

....

3. Which hurricane on the chart resulted in the most deaths?

....

4. Which hurricane on the chart resulted in the most damages in dollars?

....

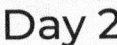

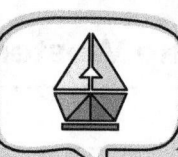
Directions: Read the text below. Then answer the questions that follow.

> Environmental disasters pose challenges to every country in the Western Hemisphere, and each nation faces unique challenges due to their geography and climate. For example, people who live near the equator are experiencing more heat waves and droughts as the climate warms. A **drought** is a long period of time without rain. During a drought, people have less access to clean drinking water and are not able to grow crops. People who live at or below sea level are affected by floods. Increased flooding is a result of rising sea levels from ice melting in the polar regions as the earth warms. In recent years, there has been an increase in storms in Tornado Alley, a region of North America where tornadoes are most likely to occur. Tornadoes require warm air to form. As the earth warms, the warm seasons get longer, and more tornadoes occur.

1. Name one way that climate change has contributed to natural disasters.

_____

_____

2. Who is most affected by droughts?

_____

3. What is the main cause of floods in places at or below sea level?

_____

_____

4. Why has there been an increase in tornadoes?

_____

_____

_____

_____

Directions: Read the text below and follow the instructions provided to complete the activity.

You have learned about some of the causes and consequences of global warming. Consider what steps people and governments could take to reduce global warming. Think about if or why governments should protect their citizens from natural disasters. In the space below, draft a letter to one of your representatives explaining what you think should be done to protect the earth and its citizens.

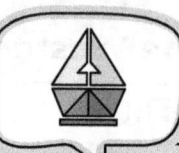
Directions: Read the text below and follow the instructions provided to complete the activity.

This week you have learned about various environmental issues that impact the Western Hemisphere. Using a search engine, research a hurricane, drought, flood, tornado, or other climate-related event that had a big impact in North America. In the spaces below, fill in the appropriate information.

Type of event:

....

Where it took place:

....

When it took place:

....

Estimated amount of Damage ($):

....

Human lives lost (if any):

....

How the government responded:

....

How long did it take the area to recover?

....

Was there anything that could have been done to prevent or limit the seriousness of this event?

....

WEEK 12

Government
Founding
the United States

This week you will learn about how the United States gained independence and analyze excerpts from the founding documents.

ARGOPREP

Directions: Read the text below. Then answer the questions that follow.

"

In previous weeks you learned about different European countries that that settled in colonies in the Americas as early as the 1500s. By 1733 there were thirteen British colonies along the east coast of North America.The people who lived in the colonies were governed by the King of Britain and had to follow the rules that he set for them. After over a century of British rule, the colonists grew tired of having to pay taxes to a King who was so far away. In July of 1776, representatives from each colony signed the **Declaration of Independence**, which was written by Thomas Jefferson. Although they were already one year into fighting the **Revolutionary War** against Britain, and had many years of fighting ahead of them, this document expressed their desire to be free. Contained in the document were many reasons why the colonists felt that they were right for making this decision, the things the King had done wrong, and the examples of the rights that all people deserved.

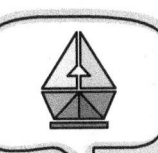
1. What were the first settlements in what is now the United States called?

   A. districts

   B. provinces

   C. colonies

   D. states

2. Which of these was not one of the original 13 colonies?

   A. Rhode Island

   B. Maine

   C. Virginia

   D. New Jersey

3. What was the purpose of the Declaration of Independence?

   A. to declare freedom from Great Britain

   B. to declare war with Great Britain

   C. to explain the laws of America

   D. to make Thomas Jefferson president

4. Who signed the Declaration of Independence?

   A. the King of Britain

   B. Thomas Jefferson

   C. citizens from each colony

   D. representatives from each colony

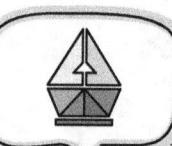
Directions: Read the text below. Then answer the questions that follow.

Yesterday you learned about the writing of the Declaration of Independence. Listed below is part of the opening line of the Declaration, followed by some specific grievances against the King. These grievances were the specific issues that the colonists had with King George III. Rewrite each of the excerpts in your own words in the right column.

In Jefferson's Words	In Your Words
We hold these truths to be self-evident, that all men are created equal, that they are endowed by their Creator with certain unalienable Rights, that among these are Life, Liberty and the pursuit of Happiness.	
He has kept among us, in times of peace, Standing Armies without the consent of our legislatures.	
For cutting off our Trade with all parts of the world:	
For imposing taxes on us without our consent.	

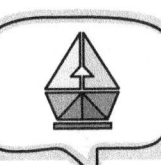
Directions: Read the text below. Then answer the questions that follow.

"

After the **Continental Army** defeated the British in the Revolutionary War, the people of America had the opportunity to start a new government. The representatives who had signed the Declaration of Independence agreed that they wanted the new United States of America to be a **democracy**. A democracy is a type of government where the people elect their leaders through voting. They also knew that they wanted a **president** elected by the people, instead of a king. Representatives from each new state came together at the **Constitutional Convention** to write the Constitution. The **Constitution** was a very large document that explained how the new government of the United States of America would be run, the new laws of the land, and the rights of America's citizens. Representatives at the Constitutional Convention had many long and important debates about how powerful the government should be. The **federalists** believed that there should be a strong central government to control the states. The **anti-federalists** believed the states should have more power to make their own decisions. In the end, the representatives agreed on many compromises, and the Constitution was signed in 1787. The states and the federal government were given a balance of powers, which you will learn more about next week.

"

1. What is a democracy?

....

....

2. Why was the Constitution written?

....

....

3. Who do you agree with more, the federalists, or the anti-federalists? Why?

....

....

....

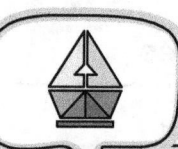
Directions: Read the text below and follow the instructions provided to complete the activity.

Soon after the Constitution was signed, the first **amendment**, or addition, to the Constitution was adopted. More amendments quickly followed. These amendments were statements about important rights and freedoms that were not already listed in the Constitution. The first ten amendments were ratified, or made official, in 1791 as their own document, called the **Bill of Rights**. Read the list below of some of the amendments. Then, answer the question that follows.

1	Freedom of religion, speech, press, assembly, and petition.
2	Right to keep and bear arms.
3	No forced quartering of soldiers in citizens' homes.
4	Freedom from searches and seizures without a warrant.
5, 6, 7	Rights to a quick, public, and fair trial by jury.
8	Freedom from cruel and unusual punishments.

1. Which of these amendments do you believe has the most impact on your life?

....

....

....

....

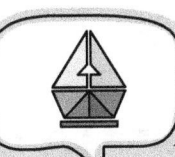
Directions: Read the text below. Then answer the questions that follow.

This week you learned about the documents that were important to the founding of The United States.

1. Name three reasons why the colonies wanted independence from Great Britain.

   A. ....

   B. ....

   C. ....

2. Would you have signed the Declaration of Independence? Why or Why not?

   ....

   ....

   ....

   ....

3. Name three important freedoms given by the Bill of Rights.

   A. ....

   B. ....

   C. ....

4. What do the Declaration of Independence, the Constitution, and the Bill of Rights have in common? Consider some of the core values and beliefs represented in these documents when constructing your answer.

   ....

   ....

   ....

   ....

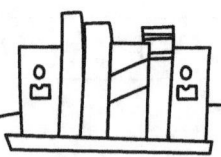

Government
The Government of the United States

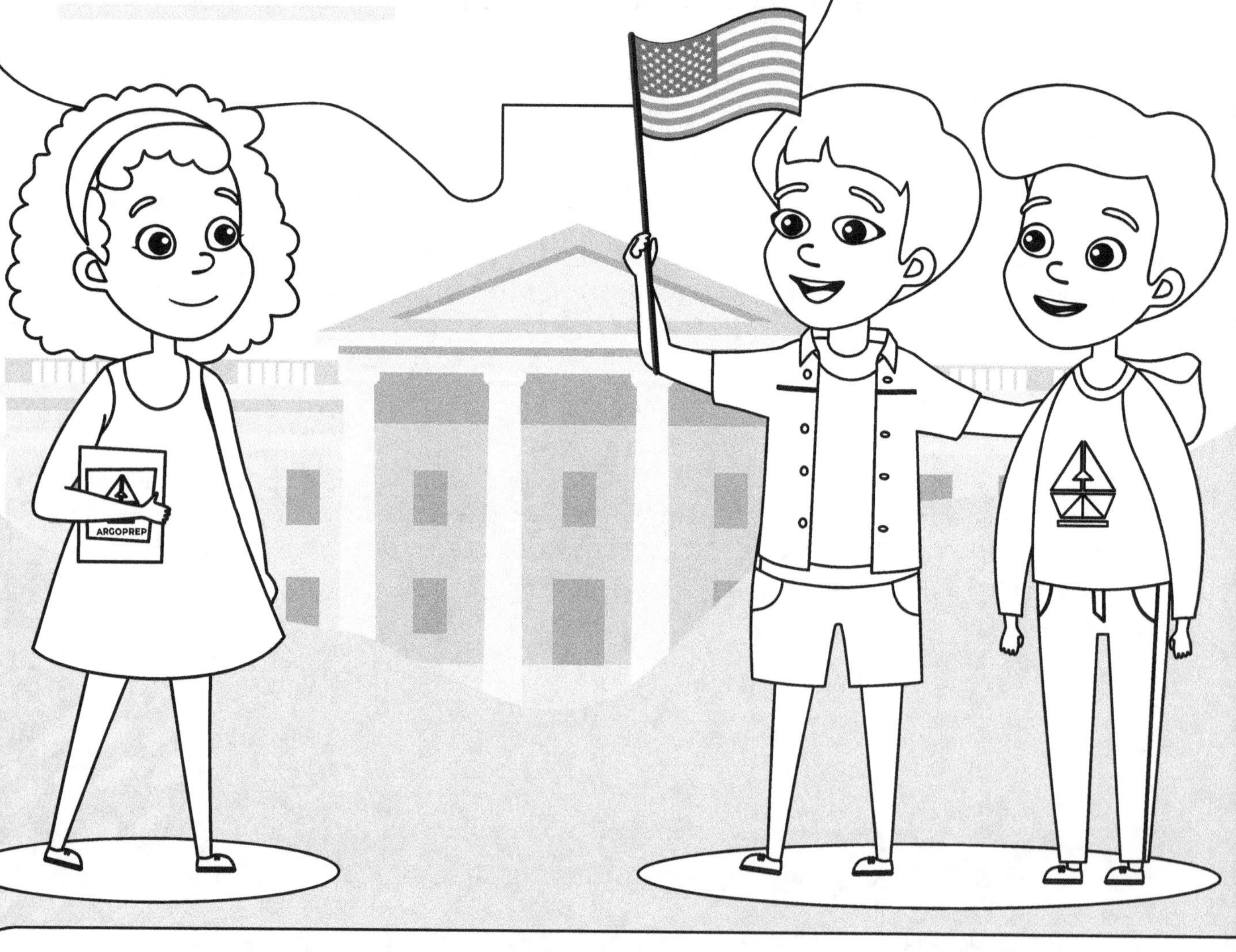

This week you will learn about the three branches of government and how they work together to create a fair balance of power.

ARGOPREP

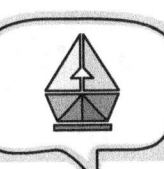
Directions: Read the text below. Then answer the questions that follow.

Last week you learned about the compromises the authors of the Constitution had to make when designing the new government of the United States. Now you will learn how these compromises worked to create a balance of power between the **federal government** and the individual states. To make sure no single part of the government was too powerful, there are three branches of government. Each of the branches of government have equal amounts of power. The **executive branch** is made up of the president and the Cabinet. The job of the executive branch is to enforce laws. The president appoints members of the Cabinet to lead certain committees and government agencies. The president is also the Commander in Chief of the armed forces. The **legislative branch**, also known as Congress, is in charge of making new laws. The two parts of Congress, the House of Representatives and the Senate, work together to pass laws. Both the House and the Senate are made up of representatives for each state, selected by citizens. The **judicial branch** is made up of the courts, headed by the Supreme Court. The job of the judicial branch is to interpret the laws and decide whether or not laws are constitutional.

1. How many branches of government are there?

A. 1

B. 2

C. 3

D. 4

2. Who is the head of the executive branch?

A. Congress

B. the Supreme Court

C. the Cabinet

D. the President

3. What does the legislative branch do?

A. interpret laws

B. make laws

C. enforce laws

D. remove laws

4. What does the judicial branch do?

A. interpret laws

B. make laws

C. enforce laws

D. remove laws

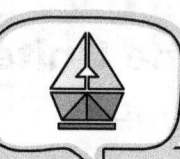
Directions: Read the text below. Then answer the questions that follow.

Yesterday, you learned about the United States government and its three branches. Today, you will look at how each branch is able to make sure the others do not become too powerful through a process called **checks and balances**. The three branches of government each have different responsibilities and are also able to "check" the power of the other branches to maintain an equal balance between them. This preserves the balance of power by ensuring that no branch can act alone.

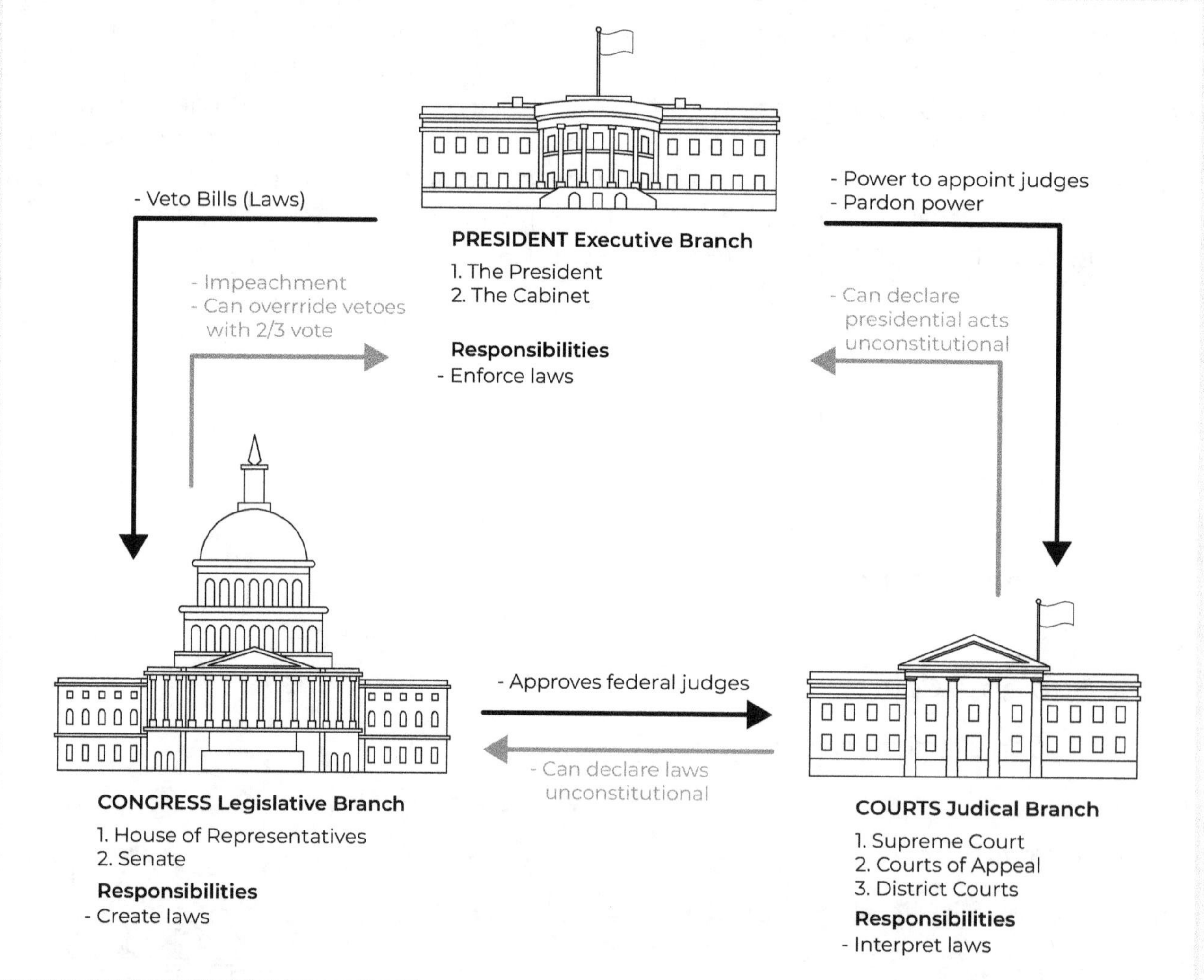

- Veto Bills (Laws)

PRESIDENT Executive Branch

1. The President
2. The Cabinet

Responsibilities
- Enforce laws

- Impeachment
- Can overrride vetoes with 2/3 vote

- Power to appoint judges
- Pardon power

- Can declare presidential acts unconstitutional

- Approves federal judges

- Can declare laws unconstitutional

CONGRESS Legislative Branch

1. House of Representatives
2. Senate

Responsibilities
- Create laws

COURTS Judical Branch

1. Supreme Court
2. Courts of Appeal
3. District Courts

Responsibilities
- Interpret laws

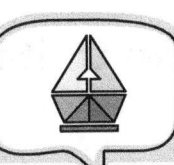
1. Which Branch of Government enforces the laws?

A. judicial

B. executive

C. legislative

D. all of them

2. What is the process which prevents any one branch from becoming too powerful called?

A. checks and balances

B. House and Senate

C. judicial review

D. impeachment

3. What is one "check" the judicial branch has on the legislative branch?

....

4. If you could be part of any of the branches of government, which would you choose and why?

....

....

....

....

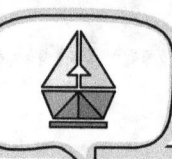
Directions: Read the text below. Then answer the questions that follow.

> You have learned that each branch of government has a special job to do when it comes to enforcing, making, and interpreting laws. Now you will look more closely at how new laws are made and approved with the system of checks and balances. Anyone can suggest a new law. New laws that haven't been approved yet are called **bills**. Any citizen can write to their representative, and that representative might write a bill based on input from the people they represent. First, the representative talks with other representatives to see if they agree with the bill. Once there are enough representatives to back the bill, the bill can be read in front of the House of Representatives and debated. Based on the debates, certain changes are made to the bill to increase its likelihood of being approved. Then, the new version of the bill is read in front of the House of Representatives. If it is approved in the House, it goes on to the Senate. If it is approved by the Senate, then it is sent to the president. The president can either approve the bill or **veto** the bill. If it is approved, it becomes a law. If the president vetoes, or strikes down the bill, the House and the Senate can vote on it again. If it passes a second time with two-thirds of the House and the Senate voting for it, the bill still becomes a law, despite the president's veto. After a bill becomes a law, the Supreme Court still has an opportunity to make a case against the law if they have reason to believe it is unconstitutional.

1. Why do you think it is important for both the House and the Senate to vote on a bill?

....

....

2. Do you think that it is fair that the president can veto a bill that has been passed by the House and the Senate? Why or why not?

....

....

3. How does the system of checks and balances affect the process of a bill becoming a law?

....

....

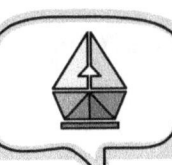
Directions: Read the text below and follow the instructions to complete the activity.

If you were to introduce a bill to Congress, what would it be? Think about an issue that is affecting your city, state, or country. Is there a law that could be passed to solve the issue? Propose your bill in the space below.

My Bill

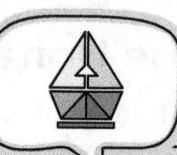
Directions: Read the text below. Then answer the questions that follow.

This week you learned about some of the important features of the United States Government, including the three branches, and the system of checks and balances between the branches.

1. What are the three branches of government?

A. ....

B. ....

C. ....

2. Describe the role of the legislative branch and the two parts of Congress.

....

....

3. How does the system of checks and balances work, and what is its purpose?

....

....

....

4. In your own words, explain how a bill becomes a law.

....

....

....

....

Civics and Government

Governments in the Western Hemisphere

This week you will learn about the governments of Canada, Mexico, and Cuba and explore their similarities and differences.

ARGOPREP

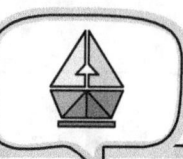
Directions: Read the text below. Then answer the questions that follow.

> Last week you learned about the United States government. This week you will learn about three more governments in the Western Hemisphere and compare and contrast them to the United States government. Canada is similar to the United States in many ways, including its language, culture, and certain aspects of its government. Canada is a democracy, but its organization is different from that of the United States. Unlike the United States, Canada never fought for independence from England. Instead, in 1867, England passed the **British North America Act**, which gave the colonies in Canada the right to form a federal government, while remaining under the umbrella of English rule. Today, Canada still recognizes the Queen of England as a ceremonial leader. However, the head of Canada's government is the **prime minister**. Unlike the American president, who can only serve two four-year terms, the prime minister can serve an unlimited number of years. Similar to the United States, Canada's government is based on a constitution. The **Constitution of Canada** outlines the structure of government, how it should operate, and how the power is balanced between the federal government and each of the Canadian **provinces**. The Canadian provinces are similar to the different states in America. They have certain rights to make local decisions, but are governed by a centralized federal government. The Canadian Constitution also features a document called the **Charter of Rights and Freedoms**. Similar to the Bill of Rights of the United States, the Charter of Rights and Freedoms outlines citizens's rights. It ensures equality for all regardless of race, national or ethnic origin, religion, sex, age, or mental or physical disability.

1. What type of government do the United States and Canada both have?
   - **A.** monarchy
   - **B.** aristocracy
   - **C.** oligarchy
   - **D.** democracy

2. Who is the head of the government in Canada?
   - **A.** the Queen
   - **B.** the prime minister
   - **C.** the president
   - **D.** the Parliament

3. Which document established Canada's right to form a federal government?
   - **A.** British North America Act
   - **B.** Constitution of Canada
   - **C.** Charter of Rights and Freedoms
   - **D.** Bill of Rights

4. Which document outlines the rights of Canada's citizens?
   - **A.** British North America Act
   - **B.** Constitution of Canada
   - **C.** Charter of Rights and Freedoms
   - **D.** Bill of Rights

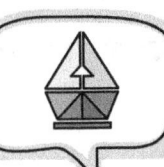
Directions: Read the text below. Then answer the questions that follow.

Yesterday you learned about the founding documents of the Canadian government. Today you will take a closer look at the structure of the government and learn some of its specific features, many of which are similar to the United States' government. The Canadian Constitution divides the government into three branches: the legislative, the executive, and the judicial. The **legislative branch** is made up of the Parliament, which includes the Senate and the House of Commons. Parliamentarians are elected by citizens to represent them and vote on new laws. The **governor general** is also a part of the legislative branch. The governor general represents the monarch of England, also known as the Crown, and gives the final approval on laws after they are approved by both the Senate and the House of Commons. The **executive branch** includes the **prime minister**, cabinet members, and other government departments decide how laws are carried out and how government money is spent so that citizens have access to the programs and services they need. The prime minister and their cabinet can also introduce bills to the parliament. The **judicial branch** interprets laws according to the Constitution of Canada to make sure that the laws are fair. The judicial branch includes the Supreme Court of Canada, as well as the provincial and territorial courts.

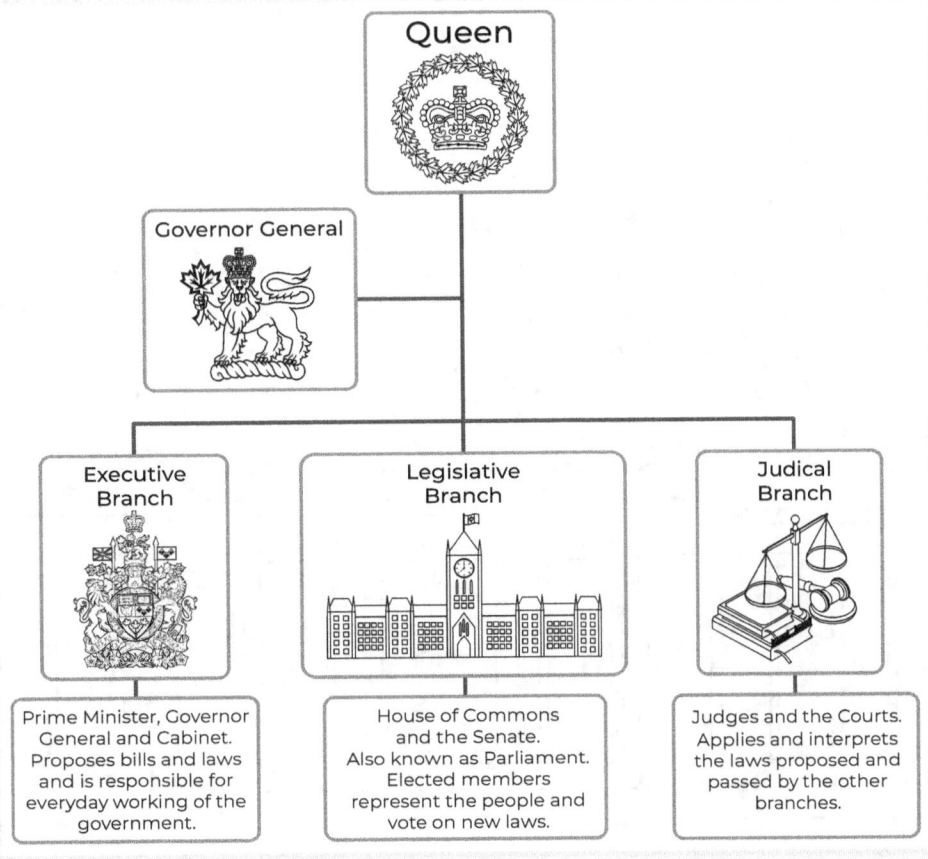

1. Who is in charge of Canada's executive branch?

    A. the president

    B. the prime minister

    C. the Senate

    D. the House of Commons

2. Who represents the Crown?

    A. the prime minister

    B. the parliamentarians

    C. the Queen

    D. the governor general

3. In your own words, explain one similarity and one difference between the governments of The United States and Canada.

....

....

....

....

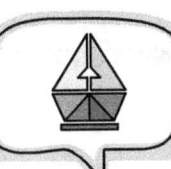
Directions: Read the text below. Then answer the questions that follow.

"

You have learned about the governments of The United States of America and Canada. Now you will learn about the governments of Mexico and Cuba. Mexico, also known as the United States of Mexico, has a government similar to the United States of America in many ways. Like in the United States, citizens in Mexico elect leaders to represent them in the government. There is a president, a constitution, as well as a three-branch government that is similar to the branches of the American and Canadian governments. Mexico is also made up of separate states that can make their own laws under the umbrella of a central federal government. One of the main differences is that the president of Mexico can only serve one six-year term, while the president of the United States of America can serve up to two four-year terms, and the prime minister of Canada can serve for an unlimited number of years, or until they choose to resign.

You have learned that the United States, Canada, and Mexico are all democracies. Cuba, an island in the Caribbean Sea, has a government that is quite different from the United States, Canada, and Mexico. Until 2018, Cuba was a **dictatorship**, or a government with one leader. Fidel Castro was president from 1959 to 2008. Then, his brother Raul Castro served from 2008 to 2018. In 2018, a new constitution was written, which limited presidents to two five-year terms. The new constitution also introduced the position of prime minister. The prime minister in Cuba is nominated by the president. Another difference between Cuba's government and the United States, Canada, and Mexico, is that the president is the head of two branches of government. In Cuba, the president serves as the chief of state and as the head of government. Many people say that Cuba is still a dictatorship. Even though citizens can vote for their local representatives, there is only one president to vote for in an election. There are also very few checks and balances within the government to keep the power of the president and their elected prime minister in check.

"

1. Name one way that the government of Mexico is similar to the United States and one way that it is different.

....

....

....

2. Based on what you have learned, do you think that Cuba is still a dictatorship? Explain your thinking.

....

....

....

3. In what country can the president/prime minister currently serve for an unlimited number of years?

- **A.** The United States
- **B.** Canada
- **C.** Mexico
- **D.** Cuba

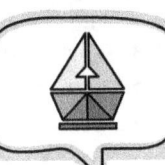
Directions: Read the text below and follow the instructions to complete the activity.

Now it is your turn to design your own government. Consider the details you learned about the different types of governments in the Western Hemisphere. Who is in charge? How would they be elected? How long can they serve? Who makes the laws? How are the citizens represented? Is there a system of checks and balances?

My Government

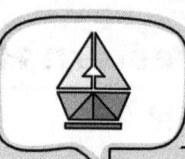
Directions: Read the text below and follow the instructions to complete the activity.

Over the last two weeks, you have learned about the governments of the United States, Canada, Mexico, and Cuba. Choose two governments that you have learned about to complete the Venn diagram below.

....

....

Time, Change, and Continuity

The Civil Rights Movement

This week you will learn about the steps that African Americans took to eliminate unfair laws in the United States.

ARGOPREP

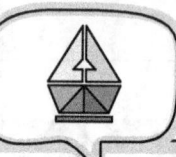
Directions: Read the text below. Then answer the questions that follow.

"When the United States was founded, the idea that "all men are created equal" was written in the Declaration of Independence. However, at the time of the nation's founding, this statement was not true. When the Declaration of Independence was written, the country was still participating in slavery. As you learned in earlier weeks, when Europeans settled in the American colonies, they used the free labor of enslaved Africans to farm the land in order to become wealthy. While England abolished the slave trade 1807, America continued to keep buying, selling, and owning slaves within its own borders. It wasn't until 1865, near the end of the Civil War, that the **13th Amendment** was ratified, ending slavery. Then, in 1870, the **15th Amendment** gave African American men the right to vote.

Still, for the rest of the 19th Century, city and state governments across the United States passed **Jim Crow** laws, which took rights away from African Americans. Some of these laws didn't let African American children go to school with white children. Other laws didn't allow African Americans to eat in the same restaurants, drink from the same water fountains, or recreate at the same parks or pools, and required them to sit at the back of the bus or train when taking public transportation. Separating people because of their race is called **segregation**. People who were prejudiced against African Americans were often violent. Many African Americans were killed by individuals or mobs, with those who killed them facing no consequences.

By the late 1950s, the struggle for equal rights and treatment of African Americans culminated in what is called the **Civil Rights Movement**. During this time period in the 1950s and 1960s, civil rights leaders organized large events such as protests, boycotts, and sit-ins as a way to push back at these unfair laws. This week, you will learn more about some of these events. After many years of fighting for fair treatment and fair laws, the **Civil Rights Acts of 1964 and 1968** were passed by the federal government. These laws made it illegal to discriminate against or refuse to sell or rent property to anyone due to their race, gender, religion, and national origin. This made all of the local and state laws that segregated African Americans illegal. While segregation is no longer legal in the United States, challenges for African Americans continue to exist in laws and in society."

1. What did the 13th Amendment accomplish?

   A. It ended slavery.

   B. It made discrimination illegal.

   C. It gave African American men the right to vote.

   D. It segregated African American people.

2. What did the 15th Amendment accomplish?

    A. It ended slavery.

    B. It made discrimination illegal.

    C. It gave African American men the right to vote.

    D. It segregated African American people.

3. What did Jim Crow laws accomplish?

    A. They ended slavery.

    B. They made discrimination illegal.

    C. They gave African American men the right to vote.

    D. They segregated African American people.

4. What did the Civil Rights Acts accomplish?

    A. They ended slavery.

    B. They made discrimination illegal.

    C. They gave African American men the right to vote.

    D. They segregated African American people.

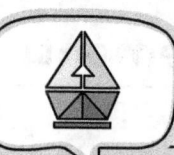
Directions: Read the text below. Then answer the questions that follow.

One of the earliest organized events of the Civil Rights movements was the Montgomery Bus Boycott. The Montgomery Bus Boycott began in 1955 and lasted for an entire year. A **boycott** is when a group of people stop purchasing or using a service. As you have learned, many states had laws that forced African Americans to sit at the back of the bus when taking public transportation. With the help of **Rosa Parks**, who got arrested for refusing to sit at the back of the bus, and **Martin Luther King Jr.**, who organized the event, African Americans refused to ride the buses in Montgomery, Alabama for an entire year. Instead, they organized carpools, or were offered affordable rides from African American taxi drivers. The city lost a lot of money in bus fares during the boycott, and eventually desegregated the buses as a result.

Another important event of the Civil Rights movement was the Greensboro sit-ins in 1960. In Greensboro, North Carolina, it was against the law for African Americans to sit at the counter in restaurants. Four young African American men who attended the local university decided to sit at the counter in protest. When asked to move, they refused. Over the next weeks and months, sit-ins spread around the country. Many students who participated spent time in jail or had to pay large fines. In the end, the sit-ins gained the attention of news stations. As a result, many cities desegregated their restaurants.

Perhaps the most well-known event of the Civil Rights movement was the March on Washington. In 1963, 250,000 people gathered at the nation's capitol to protest the unequal treatment and unfair laws that segregated African Americans and prevented them from having equal rights. There were many speeches given at the event. The most famous was Martin Luther King Jr.'s "I Have a Dream" speech, which you will read an excerpt from in the next lesson.

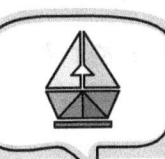
1. What was the goal of the Montgomery Bus Boycott? Why do you think it was successful?

....

....

2. Which Civil Rights event involved the most people?

....

3. Use a search engine to find out more about one of the events described on the previous page. Write one or two additional facts about the event below.

....

....

....

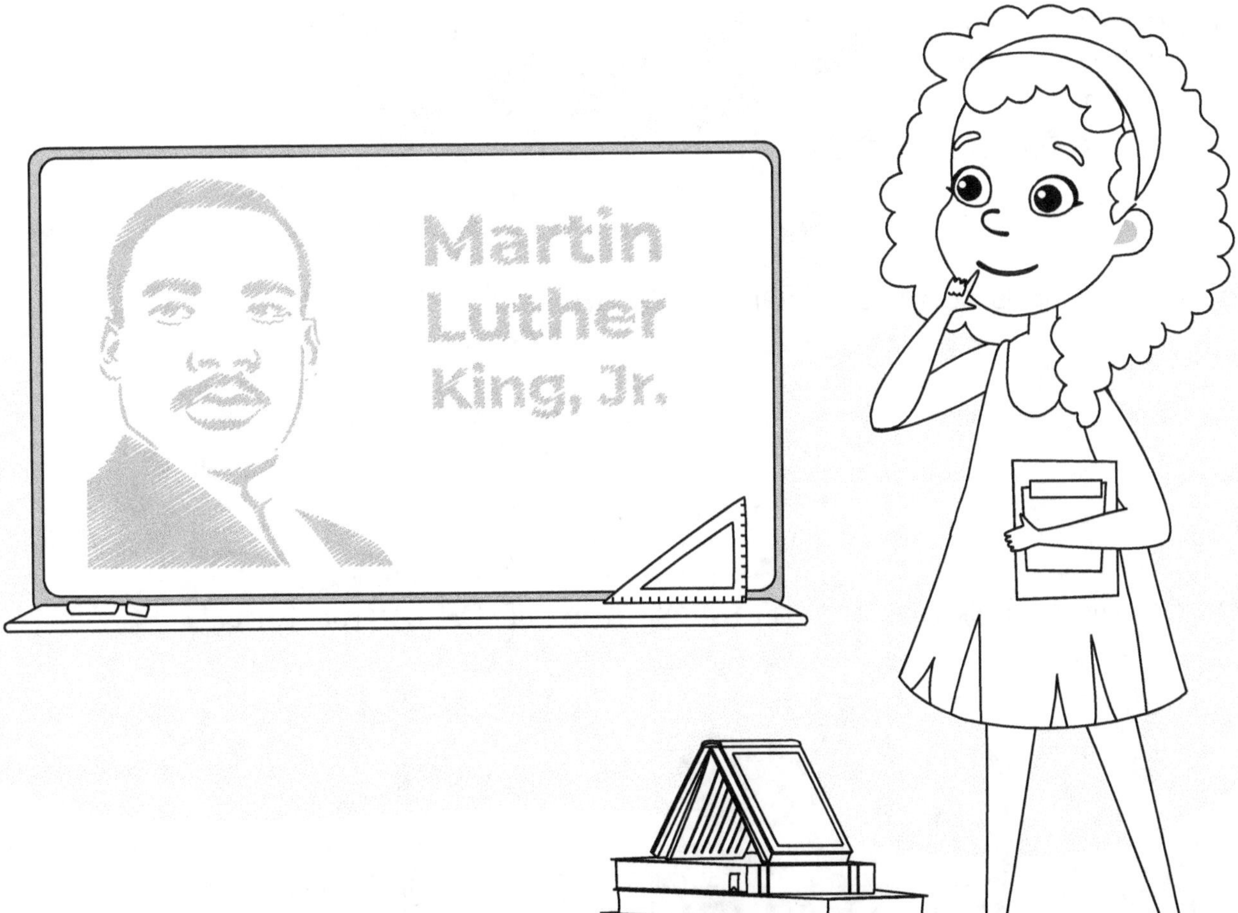

Martin
Luther
King, Jr.

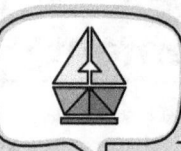
Directions: Read the text below. Then answer the questions that follow.

One of the most powerful and iconic speeches to ever have been given during the Civil Rights Movement was Martin Luther King Jr.'s "I Have a Dream Speech." King gave this speech in Washington D.C. during the famous March on Washington. Read the excerpt of the speech below and answer the questions that follow.

"I have a dream that one day this nation will rise up and live out the true meaning of its creed. We hold these truths to be self-evident that all men are created equal.

I have a dream that one day on the red hills of Georgia the sons of former slaves and the sons of former slave owners will be able to sit down together at the table of brotherhood.

I have a dream that my four little children will one day live in a nation where they will not be judged by the color of their skin but by the content of their character.

I have a dream today.

I have a dream that one day down in Alabama, with its vicious racists... that one day right down in Alabama little black boys and black girls will be able to join hands with little white boys and white girls as sisters and brothers.

I have a dream today..."

1. In 2-3 sentences, summarize Dr. King's "dream."

....

....

....

....

2. Why would giving this speech in Washington D.C. be important?

....

....

....

....

....

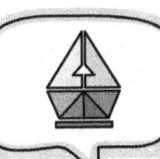
3. Do you believe that Dr. King's dream has come true? Provide evidence to support your response.

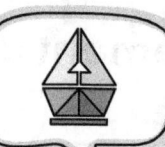
Directions: Read the text below. Then complete the activity that follows.

In 1963, the Civil Rights Movement had been losing momentum. It seemed like the movement needed new energy, and some of the leaders felt as though a "Children's March" would send a powerful message to government officials. On May 2, 1963, children left their schools in Birmingham, Alabama, and marched downtown to speak with the mayor about the racism and segregation in their communities. The police were ordered to break up the march and released police dogs and fire hoses on the children in an effort to stop the protests. The protests were shown on televisions around the country, and many people were horrified to see how the children were treated. Some civil rights leaders disagreed with allowing the children to be part of the march, while others believed it was necessary to show the country how racism was affecting America's children. Although the march was put to an end in the city, it was an important factor in convincing the United States government to pass the Civil Rights Act of 1964.

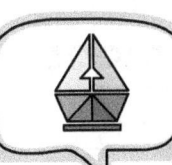
Imagine that you are a child taking part in the Children's March. Write an 8-12 sentence "diary entry" detailing why you are participating, what you experienced, what you heard, how you felt, how you were treated, and what you hope will happen as a result of the march. Include as much detail as possible.

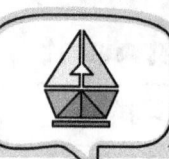
Directions: Read the text below. Then answer the questions that follow.

This week you've learned about the American Civil Rights Movement and some of its most important events. Using what you have learned, answer the questions below.

1. How many years passed between the end of slavery and the Civil Rights Act of 1964? Why do you think it took so long for all people to be guaranteed by law the rights set forth in the nation's founding documents?

....

....

....

2. In your own words, summarize one of the events of the Civil Rights movement and explain why you think it was successful.

....

....

....

3. Think about the country today. Do you think the Civil Rights Movement accomplished everything it set out to do, or do you believe there is still work to be done? Provide evidence to explain your position.

....

....

....

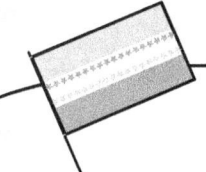

WEEK 16

Time, Change, and Continuity

The Women's Rights Movement

VOTES FOR WOMEN

This week you will learn about the actions women took to gain the right to vote in America.

ARGOPREP

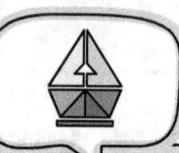
Directions: Read the text below. Then answer the questions that follow.

> When the Declaration of Independence was written, it said that, "All men are created equal." For nearly 150 years after it was written, women were not allowed to vote or run for political office. Because of this, there were no women in government making decisions or passing laws that affected women. At the time, women were not allowed to own property, go to college, or have a bank account. They were restricted to working only low-wage jobs and relying on their fathers or husbands for financial support. In 1848, 300 people gathered at an event called the **Seneca Falls Convention** in New York. The event was organized by women. One of them was Elizabeth Cady Stanton, a vocal leader of the women's suffrage movement. **Suffrage** means the right to vote. Many people gave speeches about women's rights at the convention. Stanton shared a document that she wrote, called the Declaration of Rights and Sentiments. It sounded a lot like the Declaration of Independence, but with important changes. It said, "All men and women are created equal," and listed the rights that women were not allowed to have in America. 100 people at the convention signed her Declaration. The Seneca Falls Convention started the women's suffrage movement, which involved many organized events and protests. Many states began passing laws that gave women the right to vote. In 1869, Wyoming became the first state to give women suffrage. However, it wasn't until 1920, that the **19th amendment** finally gave women across America the right to vote.

1. What was considered the start of the women's suffrage movement?

   A. the Declaration of Independence

   B. the Seneca Falls Convention

   C. the Declaration of Rights and Sentiments

   D. the 19th Amendment

2. Which of the following were women allowed to do before 1920?

   A. work

   B. vote

   C. go to college

   D. own property

3. What did the 19th amendment do?

    A. It gave women in America the right to own property.

    B. It gave women in America the right to go to college.

    C. It gave women in America the right to run for political office.

    D. It gave women in America the right to vote.

4. What was the Declaration of Rights and Sentiments?

    A. a document about women's rights and suffrage

    B. a document about freedom from Britain

    C. a document about the Seneca Falls Convention

    D. a document about the 19th amendment

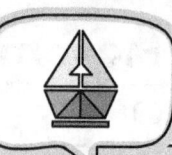
Directions: Read the text below and follow the instructions to complete the activity.

Yesterday you learned about the Declaration of Rights and Sentiments, written by Elizabeth Cady Stanton. You know that it was written like the Declaration of Independence. It included a list of complaints about the lack of freedom women had. Read the excerpts from the document below and paraphrase each line in your own words.

We hold these truths to be self-evident; that all men and women are created equal; that they are endowed by their Creator with certain inalienable rights...	
The history of mankind is a history of repeated injuries... on the part of man toward woman... He has never permitted her to exercise her inalienable right to the elective franchise.	
He has compelled her to submit to laws, in the formation of which she had no voice.	
He closes against her all the avenues to wealth and distinction... As a teacher of theology, medicine, or law, she is not known.	
He has denied her the facilities for obtaining a thorough education — all colleges being closed against her.	

Directions: Read the text below. Then answer the questions that follow.

After the Seneca Falls Convention of 1848, the women's suffrage movement grew. All across the United States, groups of **suffragists** gathered. They met to talk about how to win the vote. They planned marches and wrote speeches. They sent letters to newspapers and signed **petitions** to their local governments. However, they did not all agree about everything. Some suffragists, such as Elizabeth Cady Stanton, wanted only white women to get the vote. Others, such as Susan B. Anthony, were **abolitionsists**, who also wanted to end slavery and give African Americans the right to vote. Sojourner Truth, a former enslaved woman, was a famous abolitionist and suffragist.

In 1984, various women's suffrage groups came together to form the **National American Woman Suffrage Association**, led by Susan B. Anthony. The group's primary goal was to work together to get the United States government to pass an amendment to the Constitution, giving women the right to vote. Women had already gained the rights to vote in several states, but there was no federal law that gave all women the right to vote. This meant that depending on where a woman lived, she still may not have been able to vote, even if women in the neighboring state could. In 1917, the **National Women's Party** was formed, and its leaders, Alice Paul and Lucy Bruns organized rallies, protests, hunger strikes, and other demonstrations to convince President Woodrow Wilson to give women suffrage. Finally, on August 26, 1920, the 19th amendment was passed.

1. What was one issue that some suffragists disagreed about?

....

....

2. How was Sojourner Truth unique from other suffragists?

....

....

....

3. What methods did suffragists use to gain the vote?

....

....

....

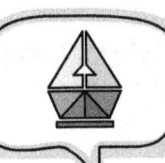
Directions: Read the text below and follow the instructions to complete the activity.

This week you have learned about the Women's Rights Movement. Think about an issue today that people might organize an event to discuss. In the space provided below, create a poster advertising a meeting, protest, or convention for your chosen issue. Include a date, time, location, and reason for your event, as well as any other relevant information that would convince someone to join the movement.

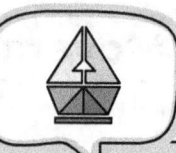
Directions: Read the text below. Then answer the questions that follow.

This week you've learned about the Women's Rights Movement. Using the information you have learned, answer the following questions.

1. Why do you think that women were not originally given the same rights as men in America?

....

....

....

2. Why is voting an important right for someone to have? What can happen if a certain group is not represented by their votes?

....

....

....

3. Why do you think Elizabeth Cady Stanton modeled the "Declaration of Sentiments" after the "Declaration of Independence?"

....

....

....

WEEK 17

Government and Civics

Multinational Organizations

This week you will learn how countries around the world and in the Western Hemisphere work together to solve important global issues.

ARGOPREP

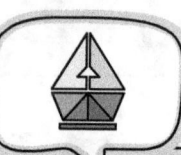
Directions: Read the text below. Then answer the questions that follow.

" While the countries of the Western Hemisphere are independent from one another in many ways, they also rely on one another. As you learned in previous weeks, all of the countries of the world are facing the same environmental issues. Apart from being a citizen of a specific country, you are also a citizen of the world. Independent countries recognize that they all deal with many of the same problems. From environmental issues to global health to world peace, countries find ways to work together to solve these issues. A **multinational organization** is a collection of countries who have agreed to work together to solve a specific issue. These organizations have many different purposes, including improving the world economy, public health, human rights, or the environment. Some examples include the World Health Organization and the World Bank. The World Health Organization is a collection of scientists and doctors from around the world who work together to keep the citizens of the world safe from infectious diseases and pandemics. The World Bank is a collection of wealthy countries, including the United States, Mexico, and Canada that work together to loan money to developing countries in order to solve problems such as poverty and hunger. Whatever their purpose may be, these multinational organizations work together with the goal of creating positive change and policies that impact citizens across the world. "

1. What is the main purpose of multinational organizations?

    A. to exclude countries who are not cooperating

    B. to promote positive relationships and solve global issues

    C. to become allies in times of war

    D. to make a trade agreement and share an economy

2. Which of the following is not a priority of multinational organizations?

    A. human rights

    B. climate change

    C. public health

    D. competition

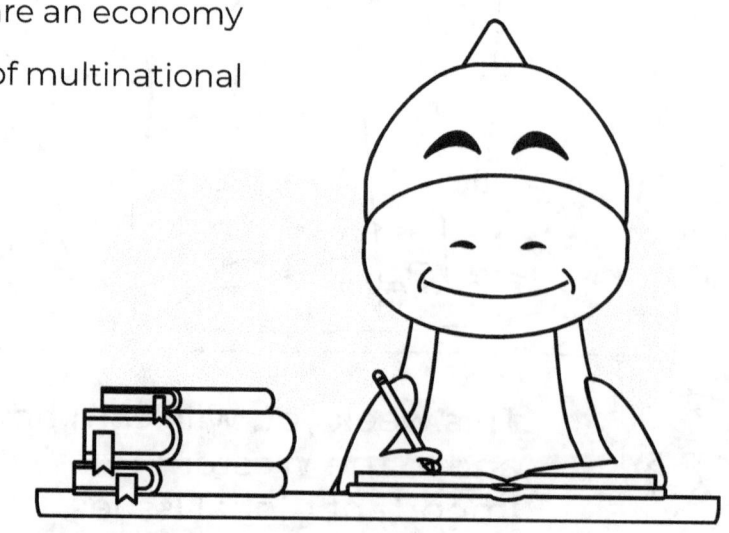

3. Which of the following would be a concern of the World Health Organization?

    A. banking regulations

    B. finding a cure for a virus

    C. a war between two countries

    D. human rights violations

4. Which of the following would be a concern of the World Bank?

    A. poverty and hunger in a developing nation

    B. a military invasion of a small country

    C. eliminating nuclear weapons

    D. solving a global pandemic

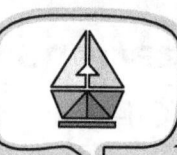
Directions: Read the text below. Then answer the questions that follow.

> The largest multinational organization in the world is the United Nations, a collection of 193 countries dedicated to world peace, cooperation, and human rights. The **United Nations** began after World War II, in an attempt to prevent any future conflicts. Read through the timeline on the next page to learn more about the problems the United Nations has solved. Then, use the information from the timeline to answer the questions below.

1. What world event resulted in the formation of the United Nations?

....

2. Which country became a member of the United Nations in 1971?

....

3. What are three issues that the United Nations has focused on over the course of its existence? Why are these issues important?

....

....

....

....

United Nations Timeline Chart

1945	Fifty nations met in San Francisco to sign the United Nations Charter.
1946	The first General Assembly met and adopted its first resolution — peaceful use of atomic energy and ending the use of weapons of mass destruction.
1949	General Assembly met in Paris and adopted the Universal Declaration of Human Rights, which stated that all humans around the world are equal and deserve equal rights and treatment.
1956	The first United Nations Emergency Force was created to manage the Suez Canal Crisis, in order to keep the peace and prevent a war from occurring.
1959	The General Assembly adopted the Declaration of the Rights of the Child, the first international document declaring the rights of children around the world.
1969	Following the Civil Rights Acts in the United States of America, the United Nations adopted the International Convention on the Elimination of All Forms of Racial Discrimination.
1971	The People's Republic of China joined the United Nations
1974	The first World Food Conference resulted in the Universal Declaration on the Eradication of Hunger and Malnutrition.
1979	The General Assembly adopted the Convention on the Elimination of All Forms of Discrimination against Women.
1980	The World Health Organization declared smallpox eradicated.
1981	The General Assembly adopted the Declaration on the Elimination of All Forms of Intolerance and Discrimination Based on Religion or Belief.
1984	The UN office for Emergency Operations is formed to help during a drought and famine in Africa.
2008	The Convention on the Rights of Persons with Disabilities was adopted.
2016	Paris Climate Agreement was adopted. 195 countries signed the agreement to reduce carbon emissions and prioritize a switch to more renewable energy options.

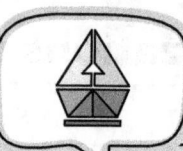
Directions: Read the text below. Then answer the questions that follow.

> Many countries in the Western Hemisphere belong to the United Nations. However, there is also another multinational organization that focuses on issues specific to the Western Hemisphere. The **Organization of American States** is a collection of 34 independent countries in North and South America. The focus of the OAS is peace and human rights in the Western Hemisphere.
>
> One of the biggest human rights issues of the Western Hemisphere is that of immigration. As you learned in previous weeks, sometimes people must leave their country and move to another in order to escape violence, poverty, or persecution. Not all countries openly welcome **refugees**, or people escaping from harm and seeking safe refuge. The refugee crisis is a big issue in the Western Hemisphere, particularly in the United States and Canada. Many refugees from Central and South America, and from around the globe, look to America and Canada for their promise of freedom and human rights. Meanwhile, America and Canada are struggling to create fast and efficient programs for welcoming and supporting refugees.

1. What is the name of the multinational organization specific to the Western Hemisphere?

....

2. What is a refugee?

....

....

3. Why do you think immigration is a human rights issue?

....

....

....

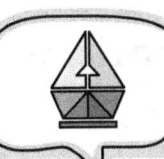
Directions: Read the text below. Then answer the question that follows.

Think about the coronavirus pandemic that has affected the international community since early 2020. Many countries attempted to work together, often through the World Health Organization, to figure out how the virus originated, what its features were, and how to best fight against the spread. Why would it be best for countries to work together to try to come up with solutions to such a complex issue like the spread of a virus, as opposed to dealing with it on their own? Use the lines provided to write out a 4-5 sentence response with supporting evidence.

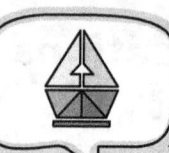
Directions: Read the text below. Then answer the questions that follow.

This week you have learned about the importance of multinational organizations across the globe, such as the World Health Organization, and the Organization of American States. Using what you have learned this week, answer the questions below.

1. What is the purpose of the United Nations?

....

....

2. What are some issues that the Organization of the American States addresses in the Western Hemisphere?

....

....

3. Explain the benefits of multinational organizations. What can you do to further the goals of multinational organizations and be a good global citizen?

....

....

....

....

History and Economics

Economies of the Western Hemisphere

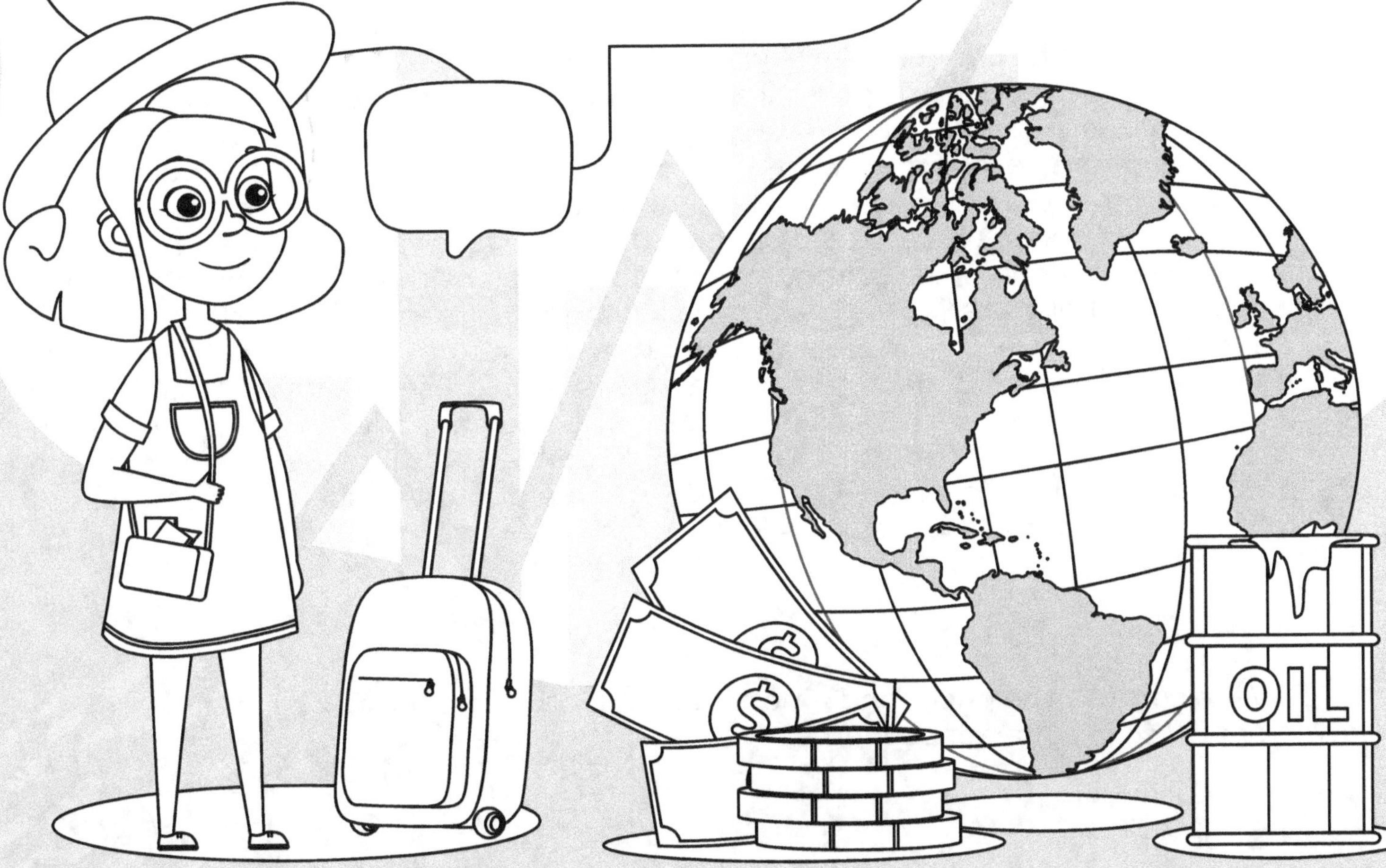

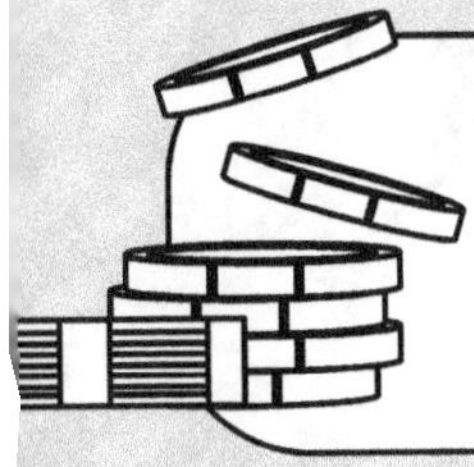

This week you will learn about the different economic systems in the United States, Canada, and Cuba.

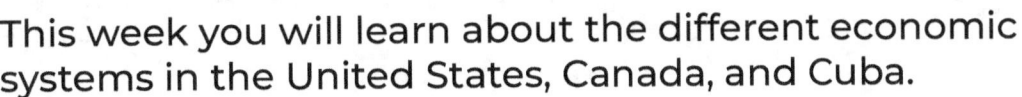

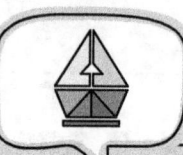
Directions: Read the text below. Then answer the questions that follow.

"

Every country has a unique economy. A country's **economy** is determined by what products are produced, how much they cost, and who controls how they are produced and how much they cost. In every country, one of the big jobs of the government is to oversee the economy so that there are enough resources, products, and money for every citizen. However, different countries have different ideas about how much the government should oversee the economy. There are two types of economies, market economies and command economies. In a **market economy**, companies are privately owned. The owner of a business decides what products to make, how many to make, and how much the products will cost. Then, they collect all of the money earned and pay themselves and their workers. One of the benefits of a market economy is that business owners are free to make decisions about their own companies. However, one of the risks of a market economy is that some business owners can make unfair decisions about how much they pay their workers or how much to charge people for their products. Without the government being able to set laws to limit the power of certain businesses, many people can be taken advantage of in a market economy.

In a **command economy**, industries and businesses are owned by the government. The government decides what will be produced, how much products will cost, and how much workers will get paid. One of the benefits of a command economy is that individual companies cannot make unfair decisions that negatively affect their workers or other citizens. However, the risk is that, if the government does not have the best interests of the citizens in mind, they can also make unfair decisions that negatively affect the economy and citizens. As you can see, neither a market or a command economy are perfect. They both have their benefits and drawbacks. This is why, in reality, most countries have a mix of both economic systems. This is called a **mixed economy**. Tomorrow you will learn more about the specific economies of different countries in the Western Hemisphere.

"

1. Who controls the prices and amounts of a good or service in a market economy?

   A. individuals

   B. government

   C. consumers

   D. everyone

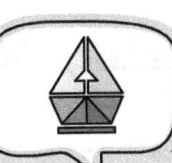
2. Who controls the prices and amounts of a good or service in a command economy?

    A. individuals

    B. government

    C. consumers

    D. everyone

3. Which of the following is a risk of a market economy?

    A. unfair treatment of workers

    B. individuals can influence the economy

    C. less products are sold

    D. more money is made

4. Which of the following is a risk of the command economy?

    A. companies are in charge

    B. less money is made

    C. the government has total control

    D. too many products are made

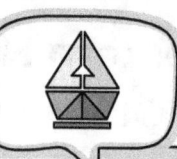
Directions: Read the text below. Then answer the questions that follow.

While the United States has many features of a market economy, it actually has a mixed economy. Even though companies are privately owned and make their own decisions about what to produce and how much their products will cost, the government has the ability to pass laws that companies must follow when it comes to things like minimum wage and other workers rights issues. However, it is not all up to the federal government. State governments also have control over how companies are run in their own state. While the federal government sets a federal minimum wage, individual states can set a state minimum wage that is higher, especially if the cost of living is high in that state. This keeps citizens protected and ensures that they can afford food and shelter. The government also provides certain services, like public education, to ensure that everyone receives equal opportunities.

The economy of Canada is similar to the United States and is also a mixed economy. One major difference is that social services, such as hospitals, are owned by the government instead of by private companies. This protects citizens from being overcharged for health care, and ensures everyone has equal access to care, even in the most rural regions of the country. Cuba has an economy that is quite different from the United States. While still a mixed economy, Cuba has more elements of a command economy than the United States. In Cuba, the government controls many of the industries, including agriculture. However, Cuba has recently introduced more laws that allow private ownership of companies. Still, the government has more control over the economy than in the United States and Canada.

1. In which country is healthcare run by private companies?

....

2. In which country is agriculture controlled by the government?

....

3. What are the benefits of a mixed economy? Why do you think most countries have a mixed economy?

....

....

....

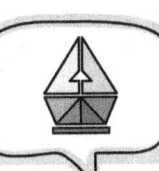
Directions: Study the text below. Then answer the questions that follow.

While geographically close to each other, Latin American and North American countries have very different economies and standards of living. The United States and Canada enjoy a higher standard of living than Central and South American nations, including the Caribbean. The wealth maps below indicate how much money the average adult has in each country. This is calculated by the total amount of wealth in a country, divided by the number of each adult.

Latin America Wealth Map 2018

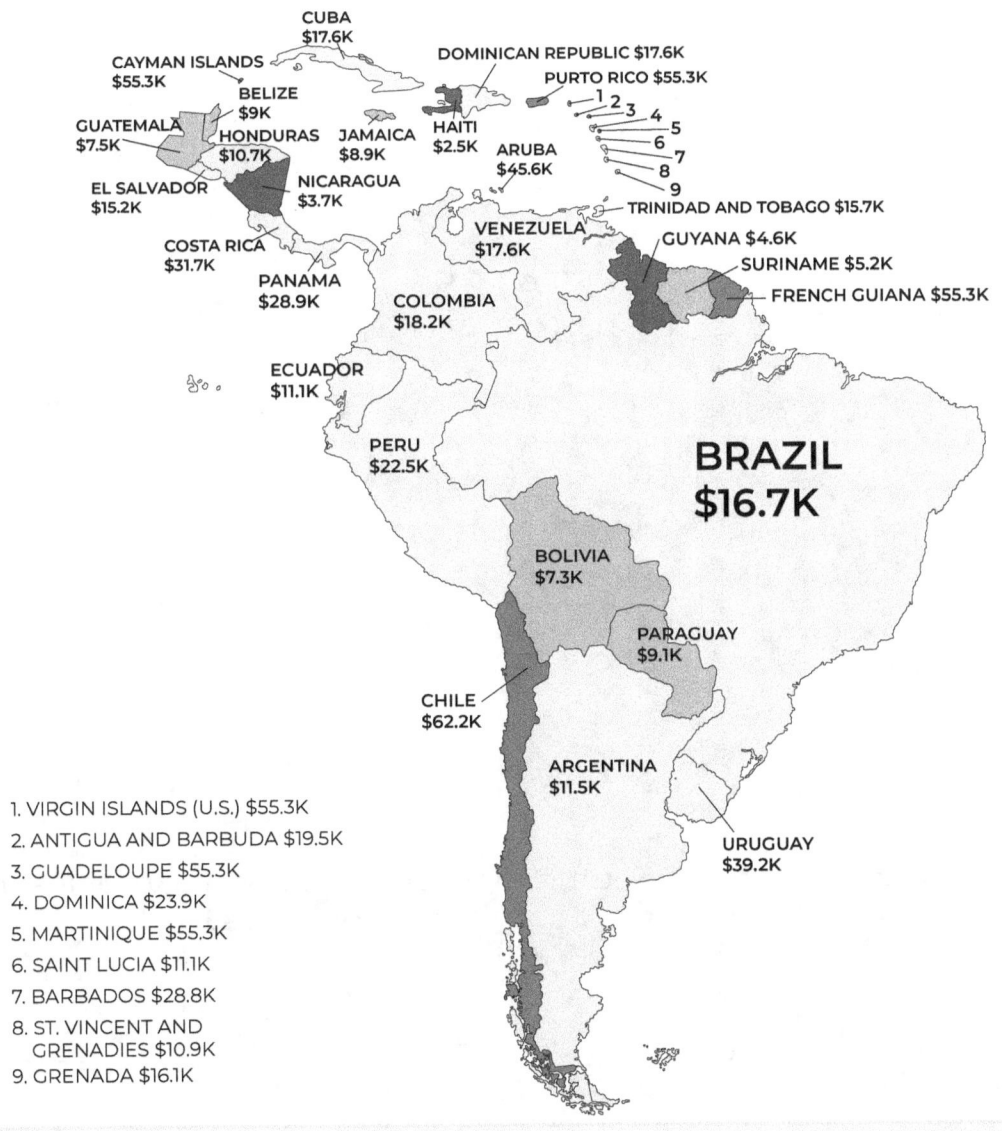

1. VIRGIN ISLANDS (U.S.) $55.3K
2. ANTIGUA AND BARBUDA $19.5K
3. GUADELOUPE $55.3K
4. DOMINICA $23.9K
5. MARTINIQUE $55.3K
6. SAINT LUCIA $11.1K
7. BARBADOS $28.8K
8. ST. VINCENT AND GRENADIES $10.9K
9. GRENADA $16.1K

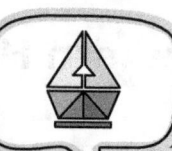
North America Wealth Map 2018

GREENLAND
$391.7K

CANADA
$288.3K

UNITED STATES
$404K

BERMUDA
$391.7K

BAHAMAS
$47.8K

MEXICO
$20.6K

1. What does the fact that many South American countries make far less money than North American countries tell you about their economies?

....

....

....

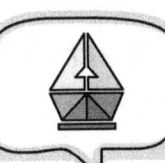
2. If people in Canada and the United States make so much more money than those in Central and South America, what do you think the price of products in those two countries would be in relation to products in Central and South America? Why?

....

....

....

3. If companies in North America notice how little workers get paid in Central and South America for their labor, what might they begin to do when they need to create new factories to produce more of their product?

....

....

....

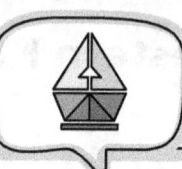
Directions: Read the text below. Follow the instructions to complete the activity.

So far, you have learned about market economies, command economies, and mixed economies. You have also learned about the economies of the United States, Canada, and Cuba. Use what you have learned about each economic system to decide where each country falls on the economic spectrum below. Place a dot and a label on the line for each country. Then, explain your thinking below.

← Market Economy   Mixed Economy   Command Economy →

....

....

....

....

....

....

....

....

....

....

....

....

....

....

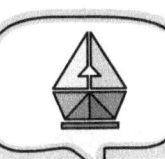
Directions: Read the text below. Then answer the questions that follow.

This week you have learned about economies in the Americas. Using what you have learned about economies, answer the questions below.

1. What are some of the benefits and drawbacks of a market economy?

....

....

....

2. What are some of the benefits and drawbacks of a command economy?

....

....

....

3. Which system do you believe is best for the most people? Explain your thinking.

....

....

....

Geography and Economics

Natural Resources in the Western Hemisphere

This week you will learn about renewable and nonrenewable resources and how each are used by different countries in the Western Hemisphere.

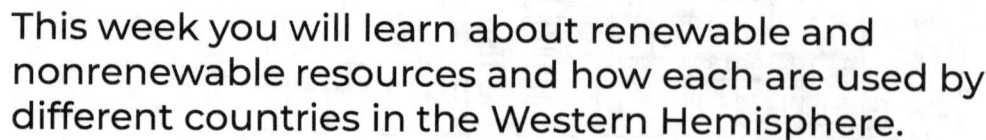

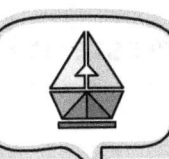
Directions: Read the text below. Then answer the questions that follow.

Natural resources are materials from nature that can be used to make the things that people need to survive, like shelter, clothing, and tools. Natural resources also include the materials we use for energy, like the fuels we burn for electricity or to run our cars, planes, and trains. People have always used natural resources to survive. However, in the last few centuries, with the human population the highest it has ever been, we are beginning to take a closer look at just how much we are using, and whether or not we might run out of resources in the future.

There are two types of natural resources. **Nonrenewable resources** are resources that we could run out of, since they are in limited supply. Coal, oil, and natural gas are all examples of nonrenewable resources. They are also referred to as **fossil fuels** because they come from deep in the earth and are very old. There is not an unlimited supply of fossil fuels, so they are nonrenewable. Fossil fuels are mostly used for energy, or electricity, and to power cars, trains, planes, and factories.

Renewable resources are resources that we will not run out of, since they are unlimited. Some examples of renewable resources include solar power, wind power, hydroelectric power, and nuclear power. Solar power is collected from the sun's rays using solar panels. Wind power is collected using wind turbines. The spinning of the turbines generates electricity. Hydroelectric power is power that comes from water rushing through turbines in a dam. Nuclear power splits atoms to create heat, which then heats up water to create steam and power turbines. Energy that comes from renewable resources is also known as **sustainable energy**, since the resources will not run out.

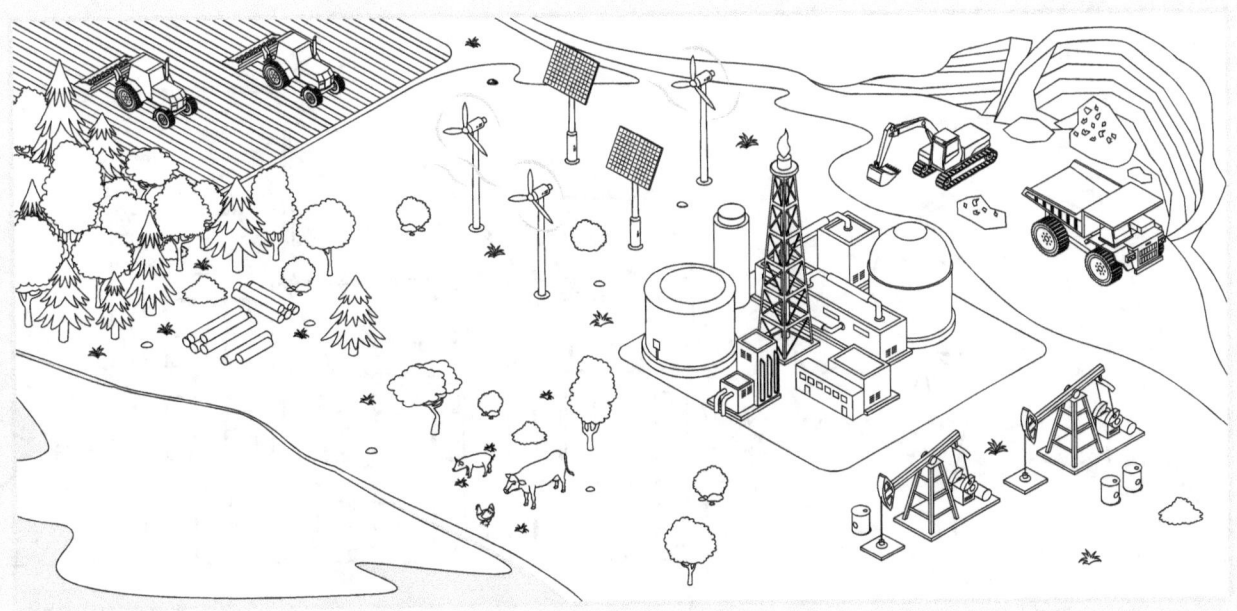

1. What is an example of a nonrenewable resource?

    A. hydroelectric

    B. coal

    C. wind

    D. nuclear

2. What is another term for nonrenewable resources?

    A. nuclear power

    B. natural resources

    C. fossil fuels

    D. sustainable energy

3. What is an example of a renewable resource?

    A. solar

    B. natural gas

    C. coal

    D. oil

4. What is another term for renewable resources?

    A. nuclear power

    B. natural resources

    C. fossil fuels

    D. sustainable energy

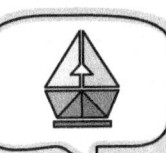
Directions: Read the text below. Then answer the questions that follow.

Some countries in the western hemisphere use more fossil fuels than others. The map below shows what percentage of energy each country uses is from fossil fuels. Countries that use more fossil fuels are using less renewable energy resources. Countries that have a low percentage of fossil fuel use are using more renewable energy resources.

% of Energy Use from Fossil Fuels

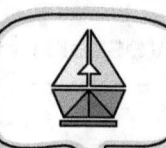
1. Name the four countries in the Western Hemisphere that use the highest percentage of fossil fuels for their energy.

....

....

2. Around what percentage of energy in these countries comes from fossil fuels?

....

3. What country in the Western hemisphere uses the lowest percentage of fossil fuels for their energy?

....

4. Around what percentage of energy in this country comes from fossil fuels?

....

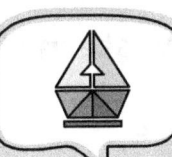
Directions: Read the text below. Then answer the questions that follow.

Yesterday, you saw how much the different countries in the Western Hemisphere rely on fossil fuels for energy. The United States, Mexico, Argentina, and Venezuela use more nonrenewable energy sources than renewable energy sources. On the other hand, Brazil gets only half of their energy from fossil fuels, and the rest from renewable energy sources. The United States harvests more oil than any other country in the Western Hemisphere. There are many oil wells in Alaska and Texas, as well as off-shore oil wells in the Gulf of Mexico. Still, the United States uses more oil than they harvest, so they also buy oil from other countries. In the last century, the United States has built many dams and wind turbines to increase renewable energy. However, the country still mostly relies on fossil fuels.

It is important to find a balance between human needs due to population growth and the limited natural resources on the planet. Aside from the fact that fossil fuels are nonrenewable, they also cause a lot of pollution. As you have learned, pollution leads to environmental issues that affect the citizens of the world. Even some industries that are technically renewable, like farming, fishing, and logging, can cause issues if not managed responsibly. If an area is over-farmed, the soil is stripped of nutrients and can no longer grow crops. If oceans, lakes, and rivers are overfished, it can take decades for the fish to repopulate. If forests are logged faster than new trees can be planted, we can run out of timber. Forests also help with global warming by recycling the carbon dioxide that results from burning fossil fuels. If there are less forests, the negative results of fossil fuels can become even worse.

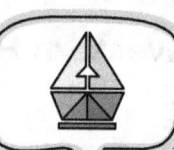
1. Why are renewable resources important?

....

....

2. Why do you think the United States continues to harvest and use more oil than other countries in the Western Hemisphere?

....

....

....

3. What is one reason that certain renewable resources, such as fish or timber, might be at risk?

....

....

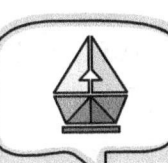
Directions: Read the text below. Then complete the activity below and the questions that follow.

Below is a list of some of the most commonly used natural resources in the United States. Sort them into renewable or nonrenewable.

Hydroelectric Power

Coal   Nuclear   Oil

Natural Gas   Wind Power

Solar Power

Renewable	Nonrenewable

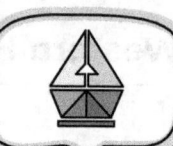
1. What are most nonrenewable resources used for?

....

....

2. What are the negative effects of burning fossil fuels?

....

....

3. Why might nonrenewable resources be so popular in the United States, even if there are many negative results from using them?

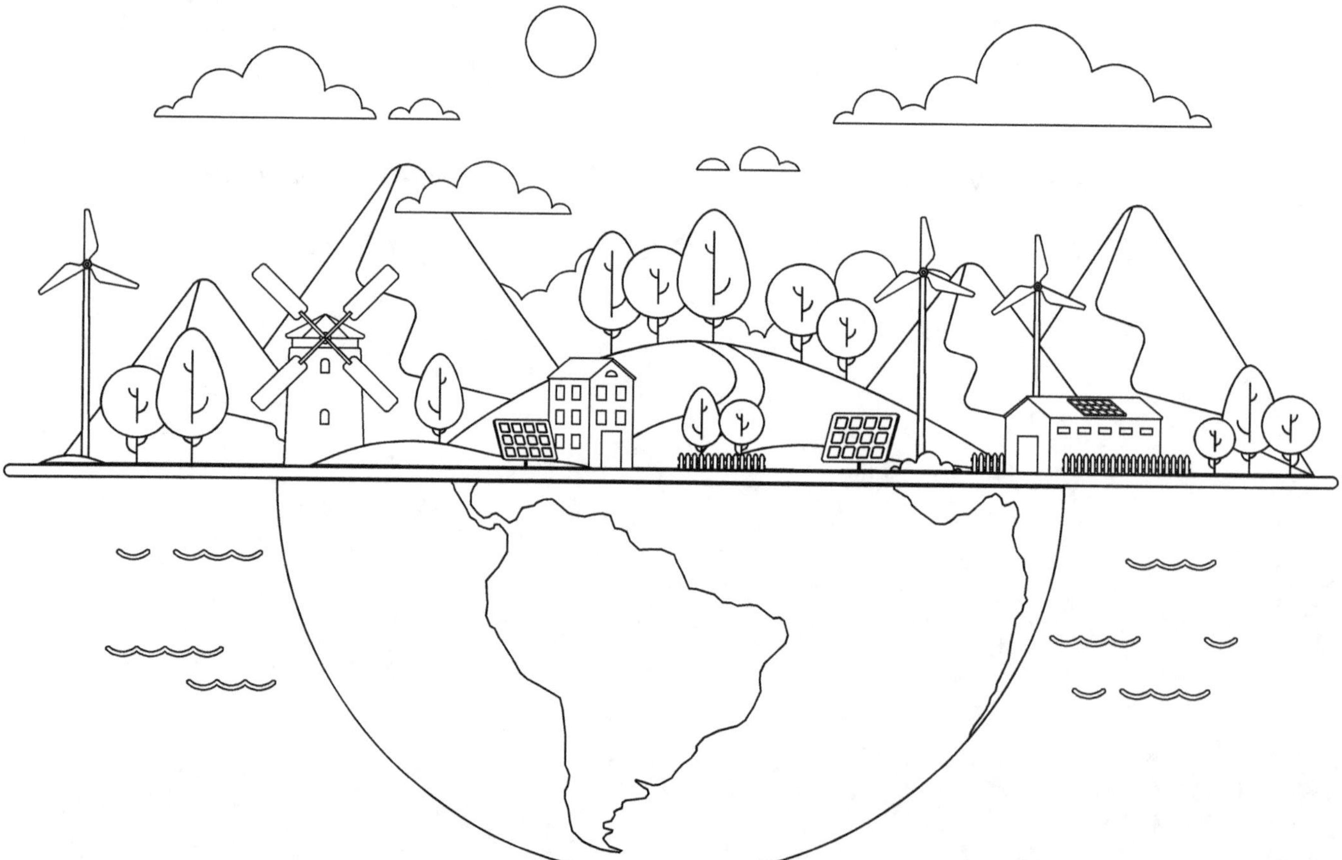

....

....

....

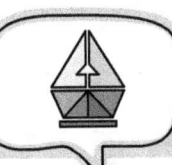
Directions: Read the text below. Then answer the questions that follow.

This week you've learned about Natural Resources in the United States and Canada. Using what you have learned, answer the questions below.

1. What might happen when the world runs out of nonrenewable resources? Brainstorm a minimum of three ideas for how a country like the United States would handle this situation.

....

....

....

....

2. How will a switch to renewable resources like wind or solar power help prevent environmental pollution?

....

....

....

....

3. Write a paragraph below answering the following question. What type of energy that you learned about this week do you think is the best for the world to continue using or start using more of? Think about things like how much it might cost to use it and its effect on the environment when you make your decision.

....

....

....

....

....

....

....

Economics

The Importance of Trade

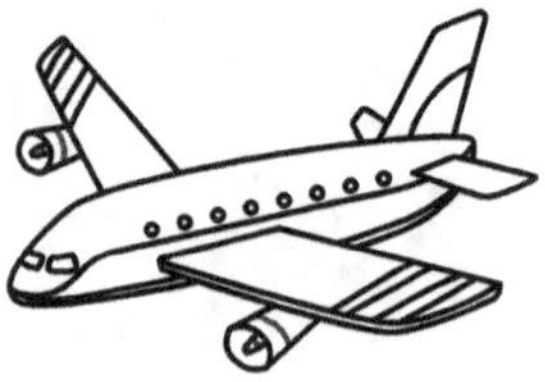

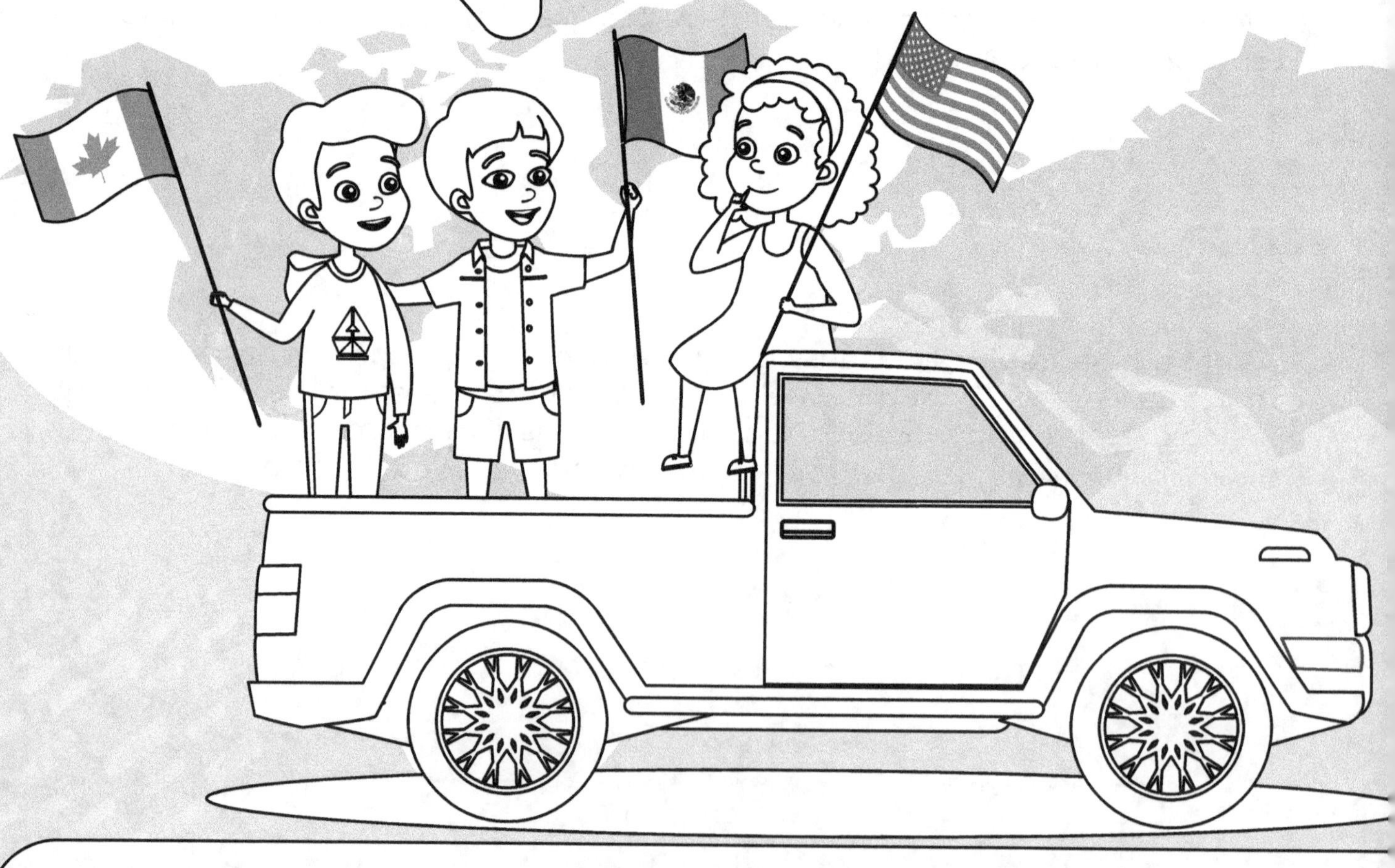

This week you will learn about the benefits of trade and how different countries work together to make fair trading agreements.

ARGOPREP

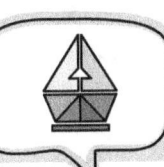
Directions: Read the text below. Then answer the questions that follow.

Think about a time when you wanted something that someone else had. Whether it was a toy or a snack your friend had in their lunchbox, you probably thought of ways to convince that person to give you the thing that you wanted. It is likely that you and that person decided on a trade. Countries trade goods just like people do. When two or more countries exchange goods with each other, this is called a **trade**. Trade is a very important part of maintaining peace and positive relationships between countries. It is also good for the economies of both countries, and can be helpful when one country has access to a material resource that another country does not have. In the Western Hemisphere, the United States, Mexico, and Canada have entered into a **free trade agreement** called the United States-Mexico-Canada-Agreement (USMCA). Free trade agreements are agreements made between countries that allow open trading between them. In the next lesson you will learn more about the USMCA and its benefits.

1. What is trade?

   A. an agreement

   B. an exchange of goods

   C. a relationship

   D. a type of economy

2. Which of the following is not a benefit of trade?

   A. maintains peace

   B. builds a positive relationship

   C. good for the economy

   D. costs money

3. What is a free trade agreement?

   A. an agreement between countries that allows trade

   B. an agreement between countries to be peaceful

   C. an agreement between countries for trade to cost no money

   D. an agreement between countries to share an economy

4. What does the USMCA promote?

   A. affordable trade between the US, Mexico, and Canada

   B. free trade between the US and Mexico

   C. affordable trade between the US and Canada

   D. free trade between the US, Mexico, and Canada

Directions: Read the text below. Then answer the questions that follow.

Benefits of USMCA	
Automotive	Automobiles must have 75% of their components manufactured in Mexico, Canada, or the United States to qualify for zero tariffs.
Agriculture	Increases access for Canada to U.S. dairy, poultry, and egg products.
Small businesses	Establishes a committee on small business issues to help firms expand trade internationally.
Labor provisions	By 2023, 40-45% of all automobile parts must be made by workers who earn at least $16 per hour.
Digital trade	Prohibits custom duties on electronically-distributed products (e.g. software, video games, movies, music, books) and supports the cross-border flow of data.
Biopharmaceutical	Raises intellectual property protections for biologic medicines in Canada and Mexico closer to the U.S. standard.
Copyrights	Protects creative works (e.g. music, movies, books) for 70 years after a creator's death.
E-commerce	**Duties** (taxes) increased for shipments from the U.S. into Canada and Mexico.
Environment	Eliminates the legal mechanism companies use to combat environmental regulations.

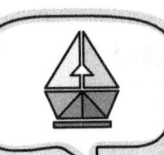
1. USMCA requires that people who make automobile parts must be paid how much by 2023?

....

2. USMCA protects creative works for how many years after the creator's death?

....

3. USMCA removes tariffs on automobiles if what percentage of their parts are made in Mexico, Canada, or the United States?

....

4. Choose one of the benefits of the USMCA from the chart and explain why it is important.

....

....

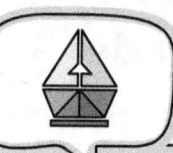
Directions: Read the text below. Then answer the questions that follow.

Trade is a vital part of every nation's economy. If a nation were to try to base their economy only on things that can be found within their borders, it would be very difficult for the economy of that nation to do well. The United States **imports,** or brings in, trillions of dollars worth of goods to their country every year. At the same time, they **export**, or send away, trillions of dollar's worth of goods to other countries, too. Some examples of goods the United States imports are oil, consumer products, food, and automobiles, while exports include those same items and other products like machinery and pharmaceuticals. Examine the chart below for more information about where the United States imports and exports the most goods to.

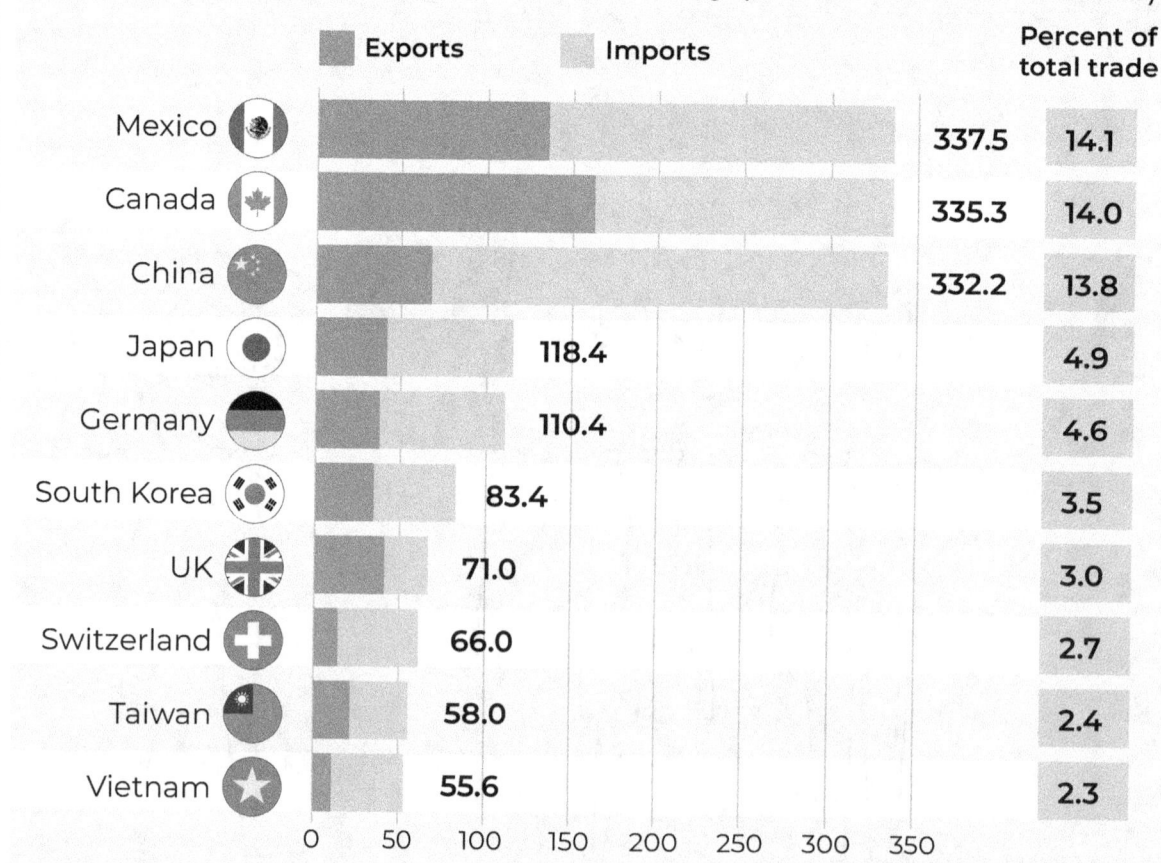

America's Most Important Trading Partners

Top U.S. trading partners for goods only (in billions of U.S. dollars)

Exports | Imports | Percent of total trade

Country	Value	Percent of total trade
Mexico	337.5	14.1
Canada	335.3	14.0
China	332.2	13.8
Japan	118.4	4.9
Germany	110.4	4.6
South Korea	83.4	3.5
UK	71.0	3.0
Switzerland	66.0	2.7
Taiwan	58.0	2.4
Vietnam	55.6	2.3

0   50   100   150   200   250   300   350

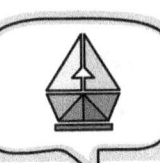
1. What is an import?

....

....

2. What is an export?

....

....

3. Which country does the United States import the most products from?

....

4. Which country does the United States export the most products to?

....

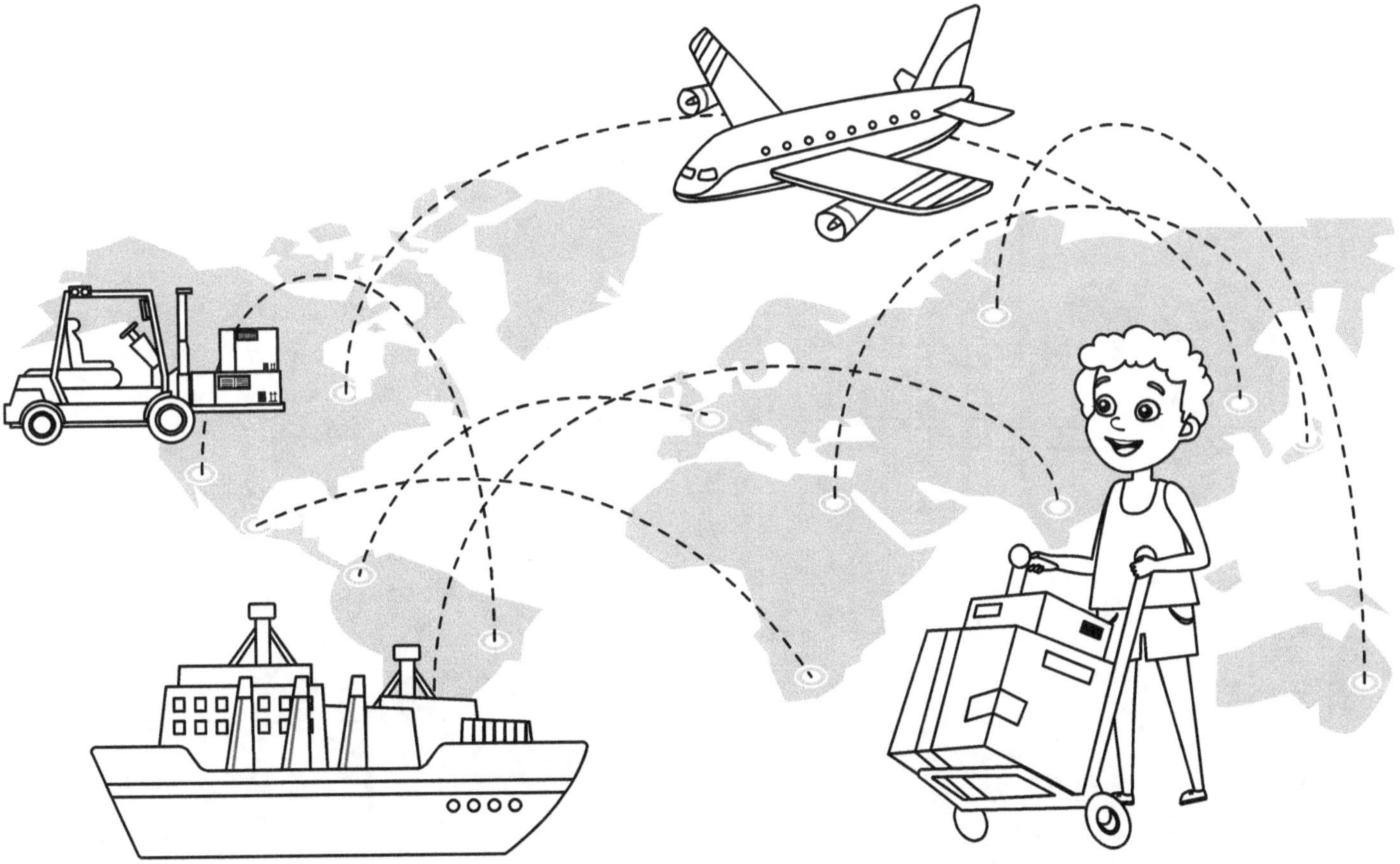

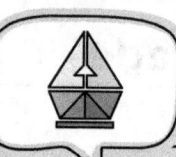
Directions: Read the text below. Then complete the activity that follows.

Countries often impose **tariffs** on goods coming from other countries in order to protect industries in their own country. A tariff is a tax placed on a product that is imported from another country. For example, if an American store wants to sell an appliance made in Japan, they will have to pay a tax on the appliance when they buy it from Japan. This means that they will ultimately need to charge more for that appliance when selling it to American customers. This will mean that companies that make appliances in the United States will be able to compete by selling their goods at a lower price. The idea behind tariffs is that consumers are more likely to spend their money on American companies, so that the money and the products will stay within the United States' economy. Look around your bedroom and your house. Look at your clothes, shoes, electronics, kitchen appliances, or any other products you own. Create a list below of at least 10 different products you found. For each item, determine where it was made, and write the name of the country next to the item.

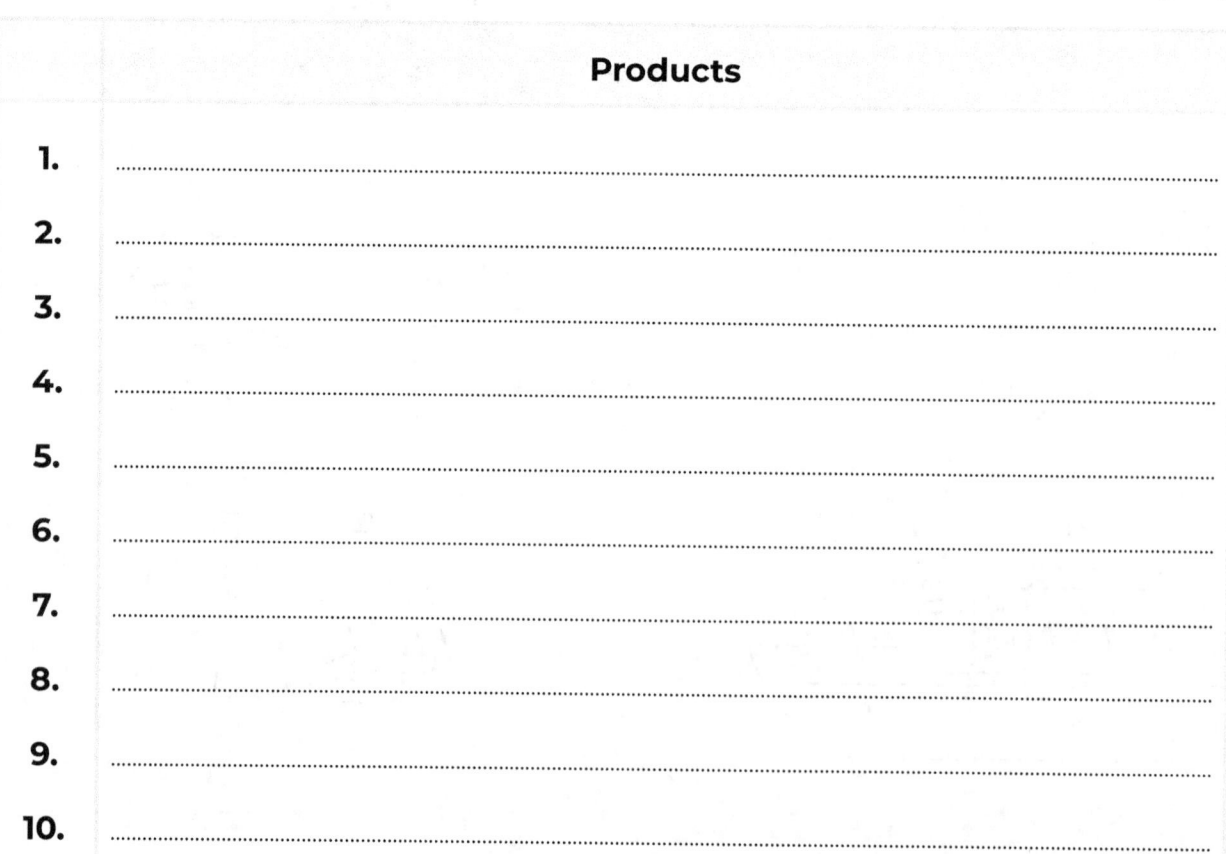

Products

1. ....
2. ....
3. ....
4. ....
5. ....
6. ....
7. ....
8. ....
9. ....
10. ....

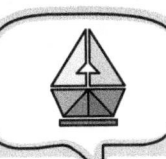
Directions: Read the text below. Then answer the questions that follow.

This week you have learned about trade in the Western Hemisphere. Using what you have learned, answer the questions below.

1. Why is it important to have trade agreements between countries? What is one benefit of USMCA?

   ....

   ....

   ....

2. What are some of the benefits of trade?

   ....

   ....

   ....

3. Do you think that tariffs are a good idea? Why or why not?

   ....

   ....

   ....

Answer Sheets

To see the answer key to the entire workbook, you can easily download the answer key from our website!

*Due to the high request from parents and teachers, we have removed the answer key from the workbook so you do not need to rip out the answer key while students work on the workbook.

 To watch free video explanations go to: **argoprep.com/social5** OR scan the QR Code:

Place your mouse over the workbook you have, and you will see the "Download Answers" button.

For detailed video instructions on how to access the "Answer Sheets," please scan this QR code.

Books explanations

📖 All Books   Grade: All ⌄   Series: Social Studies ⌄   🔍 Search...

7th Grade Social Studies: Daily Practice Workbook

5th Grade Social Studies: Daily Practice Workbook

8th Grade Social Studies: Daily Practice Workbook

4th Grade Social Studies: Daily Practice Workbook

3rd Grade Social Studies: Daily Practice Workbook

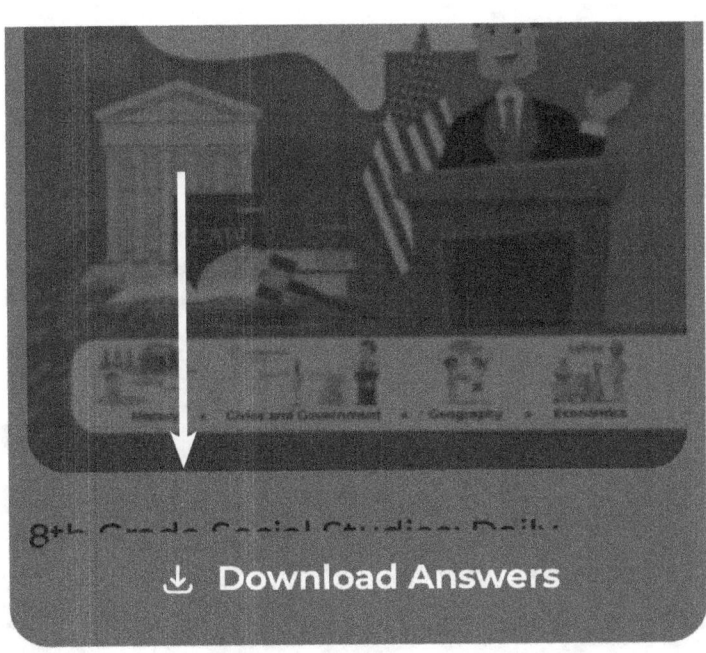

8th Grade Social Studies: Daily

⬇ Download Answers

4th Grade Social Studies: Practice Workbook

www.ingramcontent.com/pod-product-compliance
Lightning Source LLC
Chambersburg PA
CBHW081328120626
46546CB00011B/3260